"Feminist spirituality is not about women but about the possibility of human survival in a violent and blinded global system. Joan Chittister's special genius is to state issues so simply that they liberate with the liberation Jesus came to bring but which is not yet accomplished. Through poignant and shocking anecdotes, through history and theology, she shows how male-only power has distorted the minds, hearts, and faith of men as well as women, and she shows us what that perception calls us to."

— ROSEMARY LULING HAUGHTON
author of *The Catholic Thing*
and *The Re-Creation of Eve*

"Anyone who reads this book will realize what a blessing feminism is to the church and to society. Chittister's skill at identifying the structures of patriarchy in the church and in society and at demolishing the unwarranted basis for this social evil prepares the way for a new approach to human relationships and a whole new way of relating to God. This is surely a spirituality that will bring us into the fullness of what God calls each of us to be. Chittister's dynamic style of writing makes you stop to catch your breath every so often. But when you do, you are taking in the 'breath-spirit' of God."

— BISHOP THOMAS J. GUMBLETON
Archdiocese of Detroit

"After preaching in many cultures, I know that a healthy feminism is central and essential for the life and liberation of all God's people — men and women. Joan Chittister has moved feminism beyond mere power struggles to its rightful place as Gospel 101. I encourage my brothers — and sisters — to read and enjoy such liberating truth."

— RICHARD ROHR, O.F.M.
Holy Family Parish,
Albuquerque, New Mexico

HEART OF FLESH

A Feminist Spirituality for Women and Men

....

Joan D. Chittister

William B. Eerdmans Publishing Company
Grand Rapids, Michigan / Cambridge, U.K.

Novalis
Saint Paul University, Ottawa

Text © 1998 Wm B. Eerdmans Publishing Company

Published jointly in the U.S.A. by
Wm B. Eerdmans Publishing Company
255 Jefferson Ave. SE
Grand Rapids, Michigan 49503 /
P.O. Box 163, Cambridge CB3 9PU U.K.
and in Canada by
Novalis, Saint Paul University, Ottawa
49 Front St. East, 2nd Floor
Toronto, Ontario
Canada M5E 1B3

Library of Congress Cataloging-in-Publication Data

Chittister, Joan.
    Heart of flesh: a feminist spirituality for women and men /
Joan Chittister.
        p.   cm.
    Includes bibliographical references.
    ISBN 0-8028-4282-8 (pbk. : alk. paper)
    1. Feminist spirituality. 2. Women — Religious life. I. Title.
BV4527.C48   1998
248'.082—dc21   97–38367
                                                        CIP

Canadian Cataloguing-in-Publication Data

Chittister, Joan.
    Heart of flesh: a feminist spirituality for women and men
Includes bibliographical references.
ISBN 2-89088-954-8
    1. Feminist spirituality. I. Title.
BV4527.C48   1998   248'.082   C98-900134-2

A NOTE ABOUT THE ILLUSTRATOR

NANCY EARLE has been painting seriously since 1984. Born in Vermont, she inherited a love of art from her father, Edwin Earle, who himself was an illustrator. His living and painting in Arizona in the 1930s inspired Nancy's interest in the Southwest and Native American culture. A graduate of Trinity College in Burlington, Vermont, Nancy joined a Franciscan order in 1967, received an M.A. in art from Montclair State University in 1972, and taught art in New Jersey before moving to Maine in 1979.

The sixteen acrylic illustrations by Nancy in this book represent a special collaborative effort. Nancy says, "I have been intrigued by the idea of a collaboration of text and artistic images. I met Sister Joan after she had returned from the U.N. Women's Conference in Beijing and was delivering a series of lectures on women in the Scriptures and on her experiences at the conference. During a conversation we had with each other, I showed her some photographs of my paintings to explore whether we could work together. The result is this book. It has been a challenge and a privilege for me to work with each chapter of Joan's *Heart of Flesh: A Feminist Spirituality for Women and Men.*"

I will give you a new heart and put a new spirit in you; I will remove from you your heart of stone and give you a heart of flesh.

Ezekiel 36:26

TABLE OF CONTENTS

DEDICATION

....

This work,
like the rest of my life,
is dedicated to my mother, Loretta.
It was her strength, her vision, her intelligence
that demonstrated for me always
the best in both feminism and feminist spirituality
before there were words for either.

The journey to its fulfillment may be long,
but memory of her
makes all the efforts worth it.

ACKNOWLEDGMENTS

I have spent years trying to make sense out of what is now called euphemistically "the woman's question." Growing up a woman in the man's world, I had seen the effects of dualism in the life of the women in my family and felt it, even as a child, in my own. I knew that there were some things women could not do because someone somewhere had defined them as things that men did. Sometimes there were little breaks in the dike, of course: There was no boy in the family, so I got to go fishing with my father. I went to a girls' academy and held the offices that boys would have held if the school had been coed. For the four years of high school, we had a basketball team that won at least as many games as boys' teams did in other schools. But, at the same time, I knew deep down inside me, as all women do, that outside, in the larger world, men were ultimately in charge of everything. What I did not know was why. What was the origin of such ideas? And what were the effects of that kind of thinking — on men as well as on women? What were the factors, the theological foundations, the philosophical underpinnings that guaranteed to men what women were denied? The questions haunted me for years. I saw the struggle, but I could not see its resolution. And though I realized that in many situations both men and women were trying to deal with the question in open and respectful ways, the situations too often looked irreconcilable to me. Could people of good will reverse what had been named inevitable? And if they didn't, what would happen to all of us as a result?

The situation in the church was even worse. Men wrote its documents, preached its gospel, and controlled its sacraments. Women were nowhere to be seen except sometimes crawling around the floors doing the dusting. One set of virtues was defined for women, another for men, and each of them too often damaging to both.

Later, as a social scientist, I became even more fascinated by the social implications of sexism. Could something so long established possibly be wrong? Were its opponents correct when they argued that feminism was destroying the family? Was this desire of women to become more than traditional definitions allowed simply self-centeredness run amuck? Was the women's movement leading women down a primrose path contrary to their natures and so contrary to the good of the world around them?

Most of all, what did sexism, the assumption that women were naturally inferior to men, mean spiritually — both for women and for men, for the integrity of theology, for the future of the world itself?

This book is a culmination of all that inquiry, all that study. I asked the question: "What is feminist spirituality and what does it mean to both women and men?" I answered the question by looking at the values generated by a patriarchal social system and comparing them to values articulated in feminist philosophy, theology, and social theory. I asked myself what the world would look like if those values were as basic to the human enterprise as the qualities so clearly prized in the patriarchal society in which we exist. I asked what spirituality would look like if any of us really internalized a feminist worldview.

The scope and depth of such a study took a great deal of time and resources as well as support and editorial assistance. Few writers could possibly have done it alone. Certainly, not I. The list of people and places here is partial, but all were key to the culmination of the work.

First of all, I am grateful to Cambridge University and the Von Hugel Institute of St. Edmund's College, Cambridge, for the fellowship and research assistantship that made this work possible. Rev. Frank McHugh and Dr. Bernadette O'Keefe, codirectors of the Von Hugel Institute, gave this research total support from beginning to end. The Women's Forum at Cambridge provided invaluable sources and direction in the feminist philosophy that underlies any excursion into feminist spirituality.

Cardinal Stritch University, Milwaukee, and Mary Lea Schneider, OSF, president, made available the space, time, and support services necessary to the production of the manuscript. Without the personal resources available especially in the computer department at Cardinal Stritch and the special help of the library staff there, these reflections might never have seen the light of day.

One of the most astounding contributions to this work has been made by the artist-illustrator Nancy Earle, SMIC, whose work accompanies this text. Nancy read the manuscript and then responded to it visually out of her own soul and insights. She demonstrates what I feel. I am in awe of the power of her statements.

More than these, a body of readers provided the feedback necessary to the structure and tone of the text. Without their insights ideas of value would have been lost. These include Florence Deacon, OSF; Mary Frances Baugh; Brother Thomas Bezanson; Stephanie Campbell, OSB; Gail Grossman Freyne; Dr. Daniel Gomez-Ibanez; Mary Lou Kownacki, OSB; Anne McCarthy, OSB; Mary Miller, OSB; Linda Romey, OSB; Dr. Dolores Sarafinski; Gerald Trambley; and Thomas and Ann Vinca. Their deep concerns, important questions, and precise additions gave depth to the text.

Finally, friends and staff at BENETVISION: A Resouce Center for Contemporary Spirituality — my own hardworking and totally committed colleagues — did the kind of manuscript preparation that is needed to bring a long, involved text to the state of being useful to anyone in the world. To Marlene Bertke, OSB; Mary Lee Farrell, GNSH; and Mary Grace Hanes, OSB; there is no word in the English language strong enough to express the gratitude that underlies not only this but all my work with them.

To Sandra DeGroot, my editor, who bore the burden of this idea from one end to the other, and to Maureen Tobin, OSB, my personal assistant, who in very special ways makes not only this but the rest of my life possible as well, it is a privilege to make a public thanks.

Beyond these, I am grateful to the women and men who will read this text, reflect on it, and together discuss the meaning of it for their own lives. It is time in a fast-paced and profit-centered world to examine the effects of this value system on us all, men as well as women. It is readers of works such as this who make the new world we all need one day closer to the coming. I am grateful for your time and serious consideration.

Joan Chittister
December 14, 1997

FEMINISM

A CORNERSTONE OF SPIRITUALITY

There is a new question in the spiritual life: It is the spirituality of the spiritual life itself. Life here and the way we relate to it, rather than life to come and how we guarantee it for ourselves, has become the spiritual conundrum of the age. Something, we know, is missing in the match between what we have been led to believe about the spiritual life and what we come to discover that life itself is about.

This book departs from the conventions of spirituality-as-usual. A world on the brink of marital breakdown, urban violence, international conflict, and global deterioration demonstrates without doubt that spirituality-as-usual has not worked. And no wonder. When traditional spirituality requires the invisibility of half the human race, the spiritual resources of the world go bankrupt. When spirituality means private piety, the public arena is left to develop devoid of the kind of values that give heart to the world at large. When spirituality does more to underwrite a system than to challenge it, the system eventually falls under the weight of its own decay. The social signs are clear: Something is missing from spirituality as we have known it because something is missing from life as we have designed it. Women have been left out of its conceptual development; men have been distorted and diminished by its assumptions; the world has been threatened by the hierarchal implications of its conclusions.

Spirituality is not meant to be a panacea for human pain. Nor is it a substitute for critical conscience. Spirituality energizes the soul to provide what the world lacks. This book is about the kind of spirituality needed in a period when factionalism, supported by the values of the past, has reached a point of tension beyond the power of traditional spiritual priorities to cure.

1

This book on feminist spirituality for women and for men looks at life through a different lens.

Spirituality plunges us into life with an eye to meaning and purpose. When it is authentic, it is never an invitation to withdraw from life. Real spirituality, like Jacob wrestling with the angel, takes life in both hands and grapples with it. The greatest contemplatives — Bernard of Clairvaux, Teresa of Avila, Catherine of Siena, Thomas Merton — were often our most active people. The greatest activists — Dorothy Day, Martin Luther King, Jr., Mahatma Gandhi — were intensely contemplative, deeply visionary, intrinsically spiritual people. Like the Jesus who walked through dust from Galilee to Jerusalem listening to the poor, talking to women, and contending with the system, they lived deeply involved in the world and consciously immersed in an abiding sense of God. A well-developed spirituality enables us to do the same.

Deserting the human struggle in the name of the spiritual life belies the real nature of spirituality. The truly spiritual person faces every difficult question, every troublesome issue, every unresolved challenge squarely. Spirituality is not about specious consolations gained at the expense of full participation in the human race. It is about developing the courage, the determination, to commit ourselves to living all the dimensions of life with awareness and strength, with depth and quality.

There are issues in our time, as in the lives of great spiritual leaders before us, that need to be faced head on and subjected to the anvil of spirituality. The period is an avalanche of new ideas, disturbing changes, violent upheavals, and unresolved questions for which old answers do not satisfy. These very things are new grist for the spiritual mill. The temptation is to avoid the hard questions: to retreat to the past or to sit passively by, waiting for a clearer, calmer future. But that is not spirituality. That is comatose piety, at best. That is private devotion, not spiritual development, not the Christian life.

One of the major issues of our time is feminism. It challenges male-female relationships. It challenges roles. More than that, it challenges both church and state as we have known them. This rise in the consciousness of women, this description of phenomena from the feminist viewpoint of women, is changing social expectations, changing attitudes, changing families, and changing systems. It is changing spirituality, too. It is changing what we call holy, what we call good, what we call necessary.

There are some points that must be understood, however, before embarking on a reflection on the relationship of feminism to spirituality, let alone on this book. First, it is necessary to understand that *feminine* and *feminist* are not the same concept. Like *scholastic* and *scholasticism, the military* and *militarism, sex* and *sexism,* they are words the roots of which come from a common core but the meanings of which are as different as *child* and *childish. Feminine* pertains to dimensions of life commonly defined by someone somewhere to be "essentially female." It is feminine to cry, we've been made to believe. It is feminine to avoid work that is by nature grimy, we like to think — a lifetime of cleaning and scrubbing and wiping up after sick children to the contrary. Feminine is an idea, a determination we make up in our minds, too often contrary to the very evidence before our eyes. One of the major critical questions of the age, in fact, is whether *the feminine* really exists or not. [1] Some feminist theorists argue that femininity is itself a male construction used to confine women to a separate sphere and should be replaced by the notion of universal personhood, the idea that women and men are the same. Others argue that such an approach would simply turn women into men and therefore overlook the fact that there are essential differences between the sexes and that the world suffers from the loss of the specifically feminine in the public world.

This book rests on three positions: first, that what is most important is not whether the feminine is defined by society or endemic to the person but whether or not women themselves determine the content and the conclusions of those definitions. The feminine is not something that can be defined, determined, and decided by men. Women have for far too long been assigned sex roles by male authorities, and to the detriment of both sexes.

The second principle upon which this book stands is the concept that any form of dominance which leads to exclusion or underdevelopment must be exposed, critiqued, and recast if society in all its forms is to come to completion. A society built on exclusively male values and norms is a crippled society, half whole and half functioning, not necessarily malicious but certainly incomplete.

The third principle underlying this book is that spirituality itself rides on an understanding of these propositions. Spirituality that does not release the feminine dimension in both women and men leaves them half souled. That spirituality is no spirituality at all.

Feminism, on the other hand, is a point of view independent of patriarchal assumptions about the endemic and inexorable hierarchy of life from minerals to males and contrary to it, as well. It is geared to the creation of a society that rejects decisions, roles, and categories based on sex alone. Feminism regards the human race as one humanity in two genders and sets out to make the fullness of humanity available to both of them. More than that, it undertakes to release the energy of the human race. When female talents, gifts, and ideas become accessible to the human enterprise unhindered by social barriers or official limitations, then and only then, feminist spirituality maintains, will we get a glimpse of the full face of God. Feminism commits itself to the equality, dignity, and humanity of all persons to such an extent that it sets out to secure the societal changes necessary to achieve that reality for both women and men. It rests on the notion that God did not make one sex simply for the sake of serving the other and that to the diminishment of its own possibilities. The real development of the human race, the feminist contends, depends on the equal partnership of women and men, not the oppression of one for the indulgence of the other. Feminism makes humans of us all.

Feminists, it is clear, come in two genders: female and male. Life in its feminine expression is a dimension of life too little developed, true, but alive in all of us. Men know the price of its absence in themselves as well as women know the price of its being obstructed and suppressed in their personal lives. Both men and women know the toll it takes and the injustice it betokens. Feminism is, in other words, not a woman's problem; it is a human problem. Only if women and men work together, then, to stretch the human vision, to reach human possibility, can the world ever hope to really achieve it. Otherwise feminism stands doomed before it has even begun to change our worldview, to challenge prevailing attitudes, to bring us insights from the other half of the human race.

Feminism is often, of course, a different experience, a different gift, to women than it is to men. A feminist woman knows the need for and experiences the loss of feminism far differently than a feminist man does. I doubt, in fact, that to use the same word for each is exact. One is FEMinist. The other must necessarily be feMANist. One embodies the effects of a sexist society and a patriarchal tradition; the other realizes the limitations cloaked in privilege. At the same time, to say that a woman is "liberal" is no more to say that she is feminist than it is to say that a man who is pro-feminist is really feminist. To support social change is not the same as to epitomize its vision. Feminism, in both women and men, implies a change of heart. Feminism is not commitment to femaleness. It is marked only by the values we espouse and the energy it unleashes in us for the good of the whole human race. To honor women and respect men for both their differences and their likenesses is a very feminist thing. Feminism commits itself to both men and women and sees both as separate subjects, one not consumed by the other,

4

one not the norm for the other, one not the god of the other. It recognizes that both the differences and the gifts need always to be explored and never to be made captive to power and oppression.

Feminine is a female characteristic that has something to do with being gendered, with being born a particular sex, with developing traits ascribed to women by a society intent on dividing sex roles. What qualifies as feminine derives from society. In some cultures, it is not feminine at all to carry heavy packages. In other groups, carrying is precisely what women do. Feminine is what a group says it is and has nothing whatsoever essential to say about what it means to be female or feminist.

Feminism, on the other hand, is a way of seeing. It is a new worldview. It is an attitude toward life. It values things differently than did its forebears. It gives honor where honor has far too long been lacking. It looks with new respect at values traditionally held by women or called feminine, whether, as a matter of fact, anything can rightfully be labeled specifically feminine or not. It sees the world as whole only when it is both male and female, both female and male — not only in its theory but also in its shapes, in its designs, in its substance, in its daily desolations, and in its basic delights. What feminists value and do not have, what feminists need but do not receive — equality, respect, participation, resources, access — accounts at the same time for all that's lacking in the universe. Qualities derided or disregarded in culture because they are feminine are, this book will argue, the very qualities lacking in society today, the very reason that culture is teetering on the brink of its own destruction. It is time to reappraise everything we know about social quality, to balance it, to extend it, to correct its unhealthy skew.

Conventional wisdom has always insisted, for instance, that men and women do not share common human traits. Men, paragons of strength, the stereotypes insist, do not cry; women, weak and whimpering, the tradition insists, can not endure. The truth is, however, that men do cry. They cry because they hurt. They cry because they care. They cry because they can not cope with pain and oppression. The trouble is that they are told that they can not cry in public and still be called men. They can not cry out of compassion and be considered strong. They can not weep in the face of horror. They live false lives, in other words. They learn to accept stoically what should not be acceptable at all. They bridle their feelings to such a degree that, indeed, they have little if any feeling left at all. They have been well trained in the art of being half alive. And women do endure. They endure because they must. They endure through domestic abuse, they endure in pits of poverty, they endure in refugee camps, two children in their arms and one in the womb. They endure because they want to and because, deep down, whatever the culture says about their being weak, fragile, incompetent, and unable to cope, they intend to prevail over oppression, whoever they are, wherever they are. Too often they endure because they have no other choice but endurance to draw upon, and so society calls them passive. Both genders — both women and men — are allowed to be only half of what they are.

Through it all, however, men are the norm, the measure against which all of humanity is evaluated. What men say men should be determines the standard. What men are defines the pinnacle of humanity. What is good in the eyes of men for the sake of men has been judged to be good for the rest of the world, as well — whatever its effects on women. What is good in the eyes of women — for the sake of women — has been judged to be a demonstration of human weakness. But it is what is lacking in the equation, the feminine experience of the world, that the world craves. The feminist commitment to peace, freedom, dignity, respect, compassion, and mutuality have paled in the shadow of masculinist power, force, control, and domination. The Beatitudes weep at the loss, and the world is all the poorer for it.

The television sets of the world certify the lack of the feminine where we need it most. Parliaments are male. Corporation boards are male. Banking systems are male. Church synods are male. Men do the thinking for the world. Men write the laws and the decrees and the definitions. It is men's questions and men's concerns that count. They are, of course, all called universal. The thinking limps. On the one hand, a patriarchal worldview argues that men and women are essentially alike — in which case women don't have to be present anywhere; men can speak for them. On the other hand, the same argument contends that women must be barred from the public arena, from the decision-making centers of the world, from the upper echelons of everywhere because women are essentially different from men — in which case no one is really speaking for women at all.

Within the church, too, the problem is that women, though they have certainly maintained the devotions of the tradition and even influenced their development, have, at the same time, had little or no opportunity to form, to mold, to delineate, to write the spiritual canons of the faith. The theologies and spiritualities of every age have been designed or at least evaluated by men. Popes required clerics to determine whether or not the women mystics of the world were orthodox. Protestant pastors and Catholic priests burned women at the stake for daring to preach the God in their hearts.

Despite Mary of Nazareth, the Samaritan woman, the foundresses of the early churches, and centuries of holy women after them, the spiritual life has been the proper purview only of men, as have governments and economics, education and law. Women have been cast simply as consumers of the spiritual life. What women knew of the divine, the holy, the moral, the human, the social, the true has lain hidden in the reveries of mystics, the moralisms of mothers, the pious notions of nuns — never certified, never cast in theological splendor or ecclesiastical creeds. Unfortunately, that kind of deprived spirituality went long ago dry. That kind of unbalanced spirituality, strong as it is, good as it is, necessary as it is to clear thinking and intellectual commitment has seldom seemed to move the heart. Despite all the creeds in the world, we ignore the social dimensions of sin: Massacre is a public act; slavery is a public act; the repression of half the human race is a public act. It is clearly time to acknowledge the other strain of the spiritual life and hand it whole to a world whose current spirituality lies in tatters in the midst of a world fashioned on its values.

The temptation, of course, is to ignore or to resist ideas that confute the standard assumptions on which we have built our lives, however questionable their foundations, however suspect their results. The thought of feminist spirituality may, then, be difficult for some, because it implies either something they discount or something they resent. But to ignore the subject because feminism is something you fear or because feminism is exactly what makes you suspicious of anything that even smacks of the religious, runs the risk of reducing spirituality to a plastic and artificial thing, to something the spiritual part of a person can do without. Whatever impeaches life's claims, as spirituality does, requires spiritual evaluation itself.

A book like this may not give sure and certain answers to the tensions and confusions surrounding the development of a spiritual life today, but it may raise enough difficult questions to make the spiritual life different tomorrow from what it was yesterday. Anything is holier than being in an aimless rut that derives from nothing with which we can any longer identify and is going nowhere we want to go.

The important thing to note is that this book is not about femaleness. This book is about a feminist worldview, about another way of looking at life, about another set of values designed to nurture a dying globe and rescue a forgotten people. These concepts are open to men and women alike. This book, therefore, is about a way of thinking for both women and men who are tired of the carnage, sickened by the exploitation of the globe, searching, as Ezekiel promises — if we will simply go deep enough, think freshly enough, risk bravely enough — for "a heart of flesh" and a soul of steel.

Culture

I was in seventh grade at the time. My mother had cooked us an early
supper and was now sitting on the edge of her chair in the living room. I
sat cross-legged on the floor directly in front of the thing. The lights were
out, and the room was pitch black.

"Ready?" my father said.

"Hurry up, Dutch," Mother said. "Let's see it."

He bent over the thing, pressed a button, and slowly, slowly a blue-
gray light lit up the dark room, dissolved into a test pattern and finally into
a grainy, warped picture of the comedian Milton Berle, grinning wildly,
hands high above his head in front of a plain, dark curtain. It was the first
television set in the neighborhood. I could hear my mother draw in breath.
My father moved in his chair.

"This is fantastic!" I said.

"Nothing in the world will ever be the same again," my father said.

And we were both right.

The last fifty years of the twentieth century changed everything: institutions, work, lifestyles, relationships, and spirituality. Things we had never so
much as imagined before that time became commonplace. Things we had
once believed to be immutable — concepts of speed and time and distance
— passed away like snow in fog. Nothing has been the same since — or ever
will be again. Some of the changes and gadgets and inventions have
enhanced human life for some people to the very outside edge of possibility.
Some of them have also reduced other people to things, to nothing, to dust.
What happens to the spiritual life at a time like this? Some people, sensitive
to the crisis of change and fearful of the disorientation that comes with it,
want to go back and do more of what we did before and do it better. Others

want to go on, wherever the end of the road, and as quickly as possible. Clarity, certainty, surety have all vanished from the scene. Where is God in all of this? What is spirituality in all of this?

Long ago, in the desert, the Israelites discovered for all of us that the God who is God can not be substituted for by golden calves, by paltry idols that demand to be worshipped but do not satisfy. God is not a thing to be sought like some kind of spiritual trophy. The living God is the urge to life at the deepest level of our hearts. God is changing changelessness.

God is what gives life meaning and makes life bearable and draws life on. God is. And because God is a living God, present always in the here and now, life has limitless value and lasting purpose, unlimited promise and indiscernible possibility — beyond our imagination, exceeding our most audacious dreams.

And yet, precisely because God is not static, not a thing to be caged in rituals or cemented in definitions or bound into dogmas, life has dark depths and mysterious moments as well. Life gropes and ripens from one period to another in us, forever new and forever renewing, whatever our age. It is always unfinished and commonly restless. It is garnered always in part and never with fullness. We have flashes of insight and periods of awareness as life goes on, but we seldom, if ever, see the whole picture all at once. In fact, we spend most of life going from doubt to doubt, from difficulty to difficulty, unlearning today what we thought we had finally mastered yesterday so that, if we're lucky, we manage to stay young in heart and open to tomorrow.

We spend most of life trying to understand it and fail to realize that understanding life is out of the question. No one understands life. We simply grow into it. What is important is not that we strain our minds to fathom its shape and its patterns. What is important is that at the conclusion of all the theorizing we will have come to live it well.

The theology of a position like this, however, makes serious demands on those who know within themselves that life will never be complete unless the hollow in them that no thing fills is finally surfeited with what the mystics knew to be nothing and to be everything at the same time. For those who recognize that God is the magnet drawing each of us further and further into fullness of life, the love of God can no longer be an exercise in idol worship. God is the promise of life, a compulsion to new life, a pledge to more life than life can ever give us.

That means, of course, that what we knew to be sufficient yesterday may well be different tomorrow. What we absolutized yesterday may need to be unlearned tomorrow. What we took for granted yesterday may disappear tomorrow. Yet, what is at the base of the knowing is the most extraordinary knowing of all: What will not change is the presence of God, who leads us always to more and more awareness, more and more life.

Ironically, it is precisely when the life we are living begins to dry up and crumble in our hands, when what served to sustain us yesterday fails to work today, that God becomes a different kind of reality and sight becomes seeing. In those times, the God we came to know in calmer days begins to wane and fade. Old answers to new questions cease to convince. Old pieties seem either more hollow or more necessary in the face of explanations that explain nothing at all. Old understandings become embarrassing: God, we begin to realize, is not an old man on a cloud. God is not a vending machine. God is not American or Canadian or any kind of Westerner at all. God is not captured by any race, by any people, by any institution. Everything we ever thought about life, its peoples, its values, its goals begins to reel before our very faces. What once we were sure of now becomes the questions that lead us to another stage of development.

When life the gadget slips through our fingers, we begin to see life as gift. Having heaped up things and rituals and people and positions only to find ourselves still empty, still wanting, however good our motives; having discovered that the hollow place never goes away no matter how we gorge it, we look again at things we took for granted, and, if we're lucky, this time discover in them what we have never seen before. Pain and failure make astounding spiritual directors. Hurt and disappointment make amazing guides. Dislocation and rejection make spiritual creatures of us all. Uncertainty and confusion turn certitude into a consciousness of how things might be different. Then, in those times, we can't just coast anymore. We have to think things through again. We have to look at things afresh once more. We have to open our hearts and let new ideas in, new conviction in, new life in. When what is amazingly and bewilderingly new intrudes into the living rooms of our souls, it is time to realize that something wonderful has happened, yes, but that life as we knew it will also never again be the same.

The problem is that mental, psychological, and social dislocations — the kind that bring us to new insights about old truths — are too often so late in coming. We went for centuries and never questioned slavery. We made anti-Semitism a spiritual act. We theologized that the earth was the center of the universe because "man" was the centerpiece of creation. We fought "wars of religion" and never saw the irony of it all. And we do it still.

We spend so much time camouflaging reality by prettying up what we do not want to face that only when it is irrevocably unmasked do we come to see what we realize we were intended to see in the first place. We look at so many things and refuse to see them for what they really are. We look at life and divorce it from spirituality.

We have managed, for instance, to look at violence in this country for decades but failed to see its perniciousness in our daily lives. We have, as a result, in the United States and in other countries, reduced social services in order to have the money to build planes and missiles and tanks and guns instead. Even in peacetime. We have watched our educational system begin to fray because we have taken weapons for granted and preferred a strong military to an educated population. We have seen the centers of our cities go to straw because we preferred to finance defense rather than development and so made our entire society more vulnerable to forces inside the country than to enemies outside it. We have called the nuclear cancer of the world a deterrent. And we have stood by while our children roamed the streets in packs, destroying both themselves and others because violence, paraded, applauded, and institutionalized by the generation before them, is in the air they breathe.

We have made money our god and called it the good life. We have trained our children to go for jobs that bring the quickest corporate advancements at the highest financial levels. We have taught them careerism but not ministry and wonder why ministers are going out of fashion. We fear coddling the poor with food stamps while we call tax breaks for the rich business incentives. We make human community the responsibility of government institutions while homelessness, hunger, and drugs seep from the centers of our cities like poison from open sores for which we do not seek either the cause or the cure. We have created a bare and sterile world of strangers where exploitation is a necessary virtue. We have reduced life to the lowest of values so that the people who have much will not face the prospect of having less.

Underlying all of it, we have made women the litter bearers of a society where disadvantage clings to the bottom of the institutional ladder and men funnel to the top, where men are privileged and women are conscripted for the comfort of the human race. We define women as essential to the development of the home but unnecessary to the development of society. We make them poor and render them powerless and shuttle them from man to man. We sell their bodies and question the value of their souls. We call them unique and say they have special natures, which we then ignore in their specialness. We decide that what is true of men is true of women and then say that women are not as smart as men, as strong as men, or as capable as men.

We render half the human race invisible and call it natural. We tolerate war and massacre, mayhem and holocaust to right the wrongs that men say need righting and then tell women to bear up and accept their fate in silence when the crime is against them.

What's worse, we have applauded it all — the militarism, the profiteering, and the sexism — in the name of patriotism, capitalism, and even religion. We consider it a social problem, not a spiritual one. We think it has something to do with modern society and fail to imagine that it may be something wrong with the modern soul. We treat it as a state of mind rather than a state of heart. Clearly, there is something we are failing to see.

The spiritual problem of the time is the problem of denial. We live in a world where violence is rampant, where sexism is smirked at, and where economic exploitation is called good business. Either we do not see these things, or we do not call social issues spiritual questions. We have been raised to believe that spiritual questions are personal questions, that the spiritual life is a relationship between me and God rather than between me and the remainder of the universe. We maintain decent daily lives and call religious regularity goodness when the rest of the world is reeling from the new dualism between personal spirituality and public religion, between personal morality, public corruption, and corporate profiteering. Worse, perhaps, we see even humanism disappearing while the world searches on bookstore shelves for the answers to the great questions of life and the civil religion — the apothesis of secular, nationalistic, cultural values — thrives. The fact is that what we call sin may well be less what we do in our daily lives than what we are failing to comprehend about relationships in this world or, comprehending, deny.

There has to be a reason that good people can be so unaware of the relationship between the private and the public dimensions of faith. How is it that people saw no bearing, apparently, between the case of the woman taken in adultery and the system that set out to destroy her? How could it be that people sensed no dichotomy between the paralytic cured on the Sabbath and the laws that were meant to make that kind of thing inadmissible? How could it be that no one saw the disparity between the woman kneeling at the feet of the Jesus, the rabbi, and a theology that made it impossible for a woman to study the Scriptures? The reason lies in what we call holy, what we call human, what we call spiritual. These definitions have changed in every era, and not always to the good.

The concept of spirituality, the notion that all of life must be lived conscious of the divine in the mundane, is a relatively new one. In fact, the word *spirituality* itself has had a checkered history — used first in the fifth century to signify living under the impulse of the Holy Spirit but in the late Middle Ages to indicate instead a sharp division between spirit and matter. Not until seventeenth-century French culture did it again refer to a person's relationship with God and then often pejoratively and in critical response to the new quietist groups that had grown up in post-Reformation Europe. [2] Clearly, the understanding persisted that spirituality implied something special, something beyond normal Christianity. People in religious orders lived a spiritual life. Ordinary people simply kept the rules. Spirituality became ascetic athleticism lived by professional religious types. Popular religion became more a matter of legalisms, of intrachurch customs, than a personal commitment to the public facet of faith. We understood sin; we did not understand the insidious effects of attitudes that came from dualisms, clerical classes, and perspectives which were themselves in question. Thanks to centuries of oral confessions of private deviations in the Catholic tradition and a Reformation mentality geared more to personal devotion than to institutional prescriptions, the practice of evaluating virtue on the basis of individual moral measures became the norm. [3] How closely people adhered to the legal prescriptions of the faith made for the public definition of quality and character.

Goodness, popular opinion determined, showed itself in the abhorrence of personal sin, of private imperfections, as defined by systems that were themselves too often unaware of their own limited concepts of sin. The gap between the public arena and private morality grew from a trickle to a divide. Distaste for theocratic government led to a wall of separation between public principle and private piety. Religion was for private consumption. Centuries later, however, with personal standards one thing and social practice another, that kind of goodness wore thin.

In the late nineteenth century, the Vatican issued a series of papal encyclicals on social issues which began to link public and private morality. The call was both little and late, at tension with the centuries of private spirituality taught in the churches and practiced in the pews. [4] In our time, the divorce of personal godliness from social concern has obviously failed us. Piety begs for human justification, for meaning in the real world, for a purpose beyond the magical. Personal devotion is clearly not enough in a whole world full of lepers, outcasts, and disenfranchised. We have had centuries of moral checklists and private asceticisms, but the social order has continued to deteriorate as much because of them, perhaps, as despite them.

The system itself and the way we relate to it is now the moral question of the age. Now a commitment to personal insight and theological congruity and common sense becomes the spiritual challenge of our time. Maybe we should simply be asking ourselves what is missing in the world and why, instead of what is missing in our confined little private lives and why. Perhaps we ought to be asking ourselves what we are doing to make things better for other people rather than what we are doing to make things better for ourselves. Maybe we need to realize that spirituality is what we *do* because of what we say we believe rather than the pursuit of belief itself. Maybe that would be enough spirituality to change the world and to last for a lifetime.

In a situation such as this, in which one set of standards applies to personal morality and another set to the public arena, either there is something wrong with the system, or there is something wrong with the spirituality that is being developed in it, or both. We say "thou shalt not kill" to pregnant women, but we do not say it to nuclearized nations. We say that all people are made in God's image and then close whole dimensions of life to God's other image, women. We say "thou shalt not steal" in the private sector and call Third World wage packages good business. We call welfare for the poor impossible and welfare for the rich necessary. The dichotomy, the division, the double standard of spirituality pulses through life too clearly to be ignored.

Today the nature of spirituality itself is in question. Knowledge of God belongs to theology. Awareness of God is the stuff of spirituality, but that awareness is itself a spiritual discipline. [5] Every culture, every age, becomes the foundation of, is the vehicle of, spiritual awareness. Spirituality is not a purely spiritual thing. Culture functions both as a filter and as a foundation for the perception of God in the world around us. External elements in every age have shaped the spiritual responses of that time. In the early church, the clinging to Judaism as well as the need to develop peculiarly Christian assemblies which included Gentiles as well as Jews influenced the prayer life of each new community. In later centuries, the loss of the vernacular in prayer encouraged the development of the cult of the saints. Mysticism, the cultivation of a private and personal experience of God, flourished at a time when corruption among the clergy, the breakdown of the papacy, and the social disruption brought on by the plague brought the church of the Middle Ages to a point of despair and disaster. [6] Liturgical renewal as well as the loss of stable community life in a highly mobile society have shaped our own spiritual responses. And now, at the beginning of the twenty-first century, computerization, astronomy, biology, ecology, and feminism are bringing us again to look at what we believe and the way we respond because we believe it. Gone are the days of simple responses, much as we mourn them. Gone as well are the theological concerns of the past. The number of angels on the head of a pin, the number of hours a person must fast before receiving the Eucharist, the classification of "higher" and "lower" vocations have no meaning, carry no weight, hold no influence over the modern spirit. Indeed, these times demand much sterner soul than that.

It is a crossover moment in history. Not since the sixteenth century — with the growth of cities and the new social problems they created, the invention of moveable type and its influence on the spread of ideas, the development of commerce with its creation of a middle class, the discovery of new worlds with the struggles for national supremacy that attended them, and the beginnings of modern science with its commitment to empiricism — have all the major institutions of society been under so much strain. The literacy of the masses, the dissemination of information, the emergence of economic power in the hands of commoners, the uncovering of whole new racial strains, and the development of a scientific method devoted more to proof than to speculation, opened every anchor institution in society to question, to speculation, to change, to reform. It was a new moment in consciousness. God ceased to be the Great Manipulator and became the God of Jesus again, who watched and saw and waited for humankind to become more human. [7]

Theories of education changed, the nature of the family changed, the definition of human nature changed, types of work changed, philosophies of government changed, the practice and place of religion changed in both the public and the private dimensions of society. Suddenly all the givens were gone. The mindset that had driven society for a thousand years drove it no more. Theology reeled from the blow and concentrated on "proof" as the foundation of faith. [8] There were major attempts to stop change, at least to control it. Whole nations went to war in the name of religion; churches burned people at stakes; governments underwent social revolution and religious purges. Nevertheless, indexes and inquisitions stemmed neither the tide of the questions nor the transformation in the quality of the answers to them. Spirituality struggled between the magical and the mystical. The whole Western world shifted in perspective and in the practice of the faith.

And now, four and five centuries later, we are going through the same thing again. Old answers to new questions leave us staring in disbelief. Old notions of religion as a way to coax God to intervene in the daily disruptions of our fleeting interests do not impress. Old definitions of the clergy as mediators of a God who talked only to priests rather than to the sinful people in the pews fade along with the fairy tales of childhood. Old images of God as white, male, and Western do not persuade. As a result, the world is searching in strange places for strange answers to pressing questions.

Indeed, things we never imagined, things far more strange than pictures on a small screen, have happened in our lifetime. We have been to the bottom of the ocean and into outer space. We have split the atom and threatened the existence of the planet. We have decimated peoples and cloned mammals and created technical wonders. Psychology has replaced religion as a principal exercise in human development. Philosophy has encroached on theology as the arbiter of human confusion. Science has changed our definitions of God, of heaven, of life itself. Institutions are, once again, under stringent scrutiny and massive pressure to change. Nothing is stable: not marriage, not national boundaries, not economic well-being, not religion, not the globe, not even personal roles and relationships. No doubt about it: The world will never be the same again. Everything — institutions, concepts, relationships — is in flux. Nothing is the same. Why is this happening? And what does this mean for spirituality today?

The very foundation upon which spirituality has rested for centuries is itself in question.

Patriarchy

....

THE OLD WORLDVIEW

The day I'd been waiting for had finally arrived. "All those who would like to be altar servers are to report to Room 6 at 3:30 p.m.," the sign on the school bulletin board read. "All those interested," the sign said. And I was. I was in fifth grade at the time, the age of dawning possibility. Now I would be able to carry the cruets and ring the consecration bells. I would be on the altar and at the center of the liturgy. I would be as spiritual as a child could be. For years I had mouthed the same responses at morning Mass as the altar boys did. Every night in my bedroom I rehearsed the moves. This one would be easy. This one was obvious. I would volunteer to serve at Mass, and I would be chosen.

"What are you here for, Joan?" Sister Catherine Therese said when she arrived to find me sitting in her classroom after school, waiting with the boys.

"To be an altar boy, Sister," I said, totally unconscious of the implications of the language. "I already know all the prayers and all ..."

"Joan," she interrupted, "girls can not be altar boys. Only boys are altar boys! Please leave so we can get on with our meeting."

As I walked painfully, nakedly, across the front of the room toward the door, I heard the boys begin to laugh — and hoot. I will hear that sound all the rest of my life.

Spirituality is the magnet within us that draws us to God. It immerses us in a consciousness of the God who is with us and the God who is beyond us. Spirituality is a composite of those practices, attitudes, and values designed to bring us to the height of spiritual development, to the depths of goodness, to authentic conjunction with the will of God in the here and now. Spirituality is theology walking. It makes theology real. Augustine, writing about his vision at Ostia in which he discovered a sense of the presence of God, says that the moment came "with a click of the heart."[9] The ancients for all their concentration on the stages of the spiritual life were quick to teach us that it is not possible to know God, only to love God. At the end of the day, however much we study, however much we know of what we have told ourselves about the nature of God, the ancients are surely right: God is not a concept; God is a way of life.

The spiritual life, because it must be lived in the present to be real, is anything but esoteric and abstract. Culture and spirituality, in fact, are of a piece. Culture creates the framework within which the spiritual life comes to be and grow. Some people, of course, look to spirituality for refuge from the real world. They walk on the earth with their heads in the clouds. But a life that takes us out of life is no life at all. These people do not live a spiritual life; they live a spiritual fantasy, challenged most clearly by those we mark as most spiritual throughout the ages — the Benedicts of Nursia, the Francises of Assisi, the Catherines of Siena and Hildegards of Bingen, the Thomas Mertons and Oscar Romeros — all of whom got their hands dirty in the trenches of civilization. They did great things for spiritual reasons.

The notion that spirituality leads us to divorce ourselves from the culture in which we exist is a fanciful notion at best, a poor spirituality at worst. The great ascetics, even the hermit monastics, were making a direct response to the culture that bred them. They were doing what they felt the social situation demanded if what they believed about God, human nature, life, heaven, and hell was to be real in that time and that place. They were, as Walter Principe says in his definition of spirituality, simply living in ways they considered "the loftiest, the noblest, the most calculated to lead to the fullness of the ideal of perfection"[10] to which they were committed. If that ideal is confused or warped, the spirituality that follows from it will be equally unbalanced, perhaps, but not because spirituality by its nature requires disjunction from the real world. Otherwise, the Jesus who spent his life tramping through the countryside preaching to the crowds, playing with the children, healing the paralytics was not a contemplative. The history of spirituality is clear: Spirituality is belief in action.

All authentic spirituality dialogues with culture. We become what belief demands and what the culture evokes. When the two are in harmony — when the way we respond to institutions comes out of what we believe about the theology of authority, for instance — the result is a government that mirrors those religious ideas. Consequently, the effects range from the development of the theocratic state in the High Middle Ages — when church and state were one — to the cultivation in another time of civil religion, of a democracy where citizens hallow the state because they themselves have created it and they themselves have given it the power it wields over them.

The belief that all authority came from God and was passed down through defined channels — from pope to king to vassal to serf, "the king of his own castle" — made submission, whatever the consequences, whatever the sense of it, a logical spiritual response to a theology of power that made authority figures vicars of the divine. When growing attention to the role of free will and reason shifted emphasis away from the idea of the divine designation of absolute power to the development of national states through the consensus of the people, republican government received theological legitimacy. Nevertheless, the notion of the scarcity of power remained, despite the fall of monarchy. Some people in the West, for the most part white males with assets and education, had the right to power, and others did not. It was that simple. The Catholic Church held until Vatican II, at least officially, that freedom of conscience defied the sacred preeminence of authority; that, as Pope Pius IX taught, "error" — meaning other viewpoints — had no rights; that pluralism in government was a moral fallacy; and that church and state should be one so that Truth would reign. [11]

That kind of thinking translated into propositions that entitled some to rule and cut the rest of the world off at the base with little recourse and less right. Because some people for some reason had direct power from God, they could do whatever they liked with it, and they were beholden to no one but themselves. Others were by nature required to obey. To accept the first statement — that some are entitled by nature or role or social place — is to accept, to require, domination and powerlessness as well. To develop a theology of divine right is simply prelude to the creation of an absolutist state. It is, furthermore, to accept a vision of society which at its operational center is at best only partial, only male. It is to create a world that walks on one leg, sees with one eye, and thinks with only one side of its mind.

The theocratic state grew out of a culture that assumed the divine right of kings. From that belief everything else followed: Absolutism was its handmaid, and authoritarianism its stock in trade. Governments depended on it, clericalism thrived on it, relationships were defined by it, and the spiritual life of individuals was molded by it. In this environment blind obedience became the height of spiritual achievement. Everyone suffered from the loss of autonomy, of course, but women most of all.

On the other hand, in societies where, by virtue of a social contract, the people voluntarily relinquish their personal authority to the state for the good of the whole, the state also requires tribute. The structures are different, perhaps, but the effects are the same: Some people hold power, and all other people are subject to it. The theological question is: Who are entitled to hold this power? And how do they get it? And who said so? Clearly, women hold little influence, almost no authority, and only minimal positions. The exceptions to the rule — Queen Elizabeth I, Golda Meir, Margaret Thatcher — prove it by their rarity. Men have power by nature, of course, but not all of them get it, or they get it only over women and children. Why? And what does this mean for the spiritual life of both men and women?

There is certainly nothing endemically wrong with the proposition that some people have power and some people don't. The problem lies primarily in the manner of achieving power and the practice of distributing it. That question, though, is precisely the point at which, in our time, spiritualities have begun to clash. The assumptions about who gets power — who decides and defines and directs this world and everything in it — and how that power devolves undergird an entire pattern of thought, theological and social. That control, long theologized, long exercised, and long regarded as natural, is now under intense scrutiny and unrelenting question. Both its tenets and its effects stand in dispute.

Multiple variations on the power theme have been demonstrated across history, but all of them come down, ultimately, to the same thing: There are those who have the right to authority and those who do not, and they all know who they are because theology and philosophy have taught them so.

But *what* theology and *what* philosophy? How did we arrive at the notion that some people are born worth listening to and others are not? The ideas are tangled but consistent.

Theologians from the time of Augustine, interpreting Scripture on the basis of then-contemporary understandings, said that men, males, were the crown of creation, the pinnacle of life. Everything else in nature ranked below them. Women, too, were made in the image of God, of course — at least if they were joined to a man — but that image, the philosophers and theologians argued, blurred a bit under the impact of biology. [12] Women obviously were created to give birth — a very animal, earthy, natural thing — while men, since they were clearly not created to give birth but only to capacitate it, were obviously made to think and to create — a very divine thing. The implications were clear: Women were earthy and natural; men were reasonable and spiritual. The correlation was beyond doubt: God, pure reason and omniscient creator, had to be male. [13] As one wag wrote, "First God created man, and then man created God." And the wag was right. The implications for society of the insistence on the maleness of a God who is more defined as Lord of Hosts, King of Heaven, and Father than as pure spirit, as Sophia wisdom, as the one who claims "I am who am" can hardly be overestimated.

How prior notions of women's birthing powers, exalted — even worshipped — in early societies, came to be displaced by male gods and male ideals remains a matter of anthropological debate and discovery. Some say by force; some say by changes in the nature of society. [14] One thing is sure, however. Greek philosophers attached greater value to the mind than to the body. Incorporeal and spiritual, the mind — the soul — they reasoned, would not, could not, die. Its very immortality attested to its superiority. [15] Bodies, on the other hand, were corruptible, disposable, mortal in the most ultimate sense of the word. Bodies were ultimately worthless.

Bodies, with their drives and needs, their impulses and urges, warranted basic distrust by virtue of their threat to right reasoning, if nothing else. And women, most of all, the blatantly natural, the totally carnal, the most bodily of bodies, epitomized the hazard and jeopardized the rationality of the male soul. If men responded to the presence of a woman spontaneously, then the way to protect the soul of the man from distraction, irrationality, and sin was to keep women out of sight, out of mind. Women's bodies were dangerous to men, dangerous to thought, dangerous to society, dangerous to religion. [16] To have women in the public arena, the marketplace of ideas, threatened the system itself. Women were a different species of humanity, a lower species, a special nature, the same as man — but different. [17] Woman became caught in a spirituality of contradictions. Woman by nature was not a spiritual being. She was human but not reasonable ("women are so emotional"), human but inferior ("girls can't do math"), human but naturally weak ("a woman can't run marathons"), human but incapable of self-direction (women, like children, don't have legal rights). And, if she couldn't direct herself, she surely couldn't direct anybody else either. In some earlier Western societies, even her boy children were removed from her direction at the age of twelve, and in many societies of the world today, they still are.

This continuing war against the body was a bitter and a brutal one. Spiritualities from Gnosticism to Jansenism abounded, far into the twentieth century, intent on the suppression of physical needs, physical pleasure, physical joy, and physical reality. Women's bodies in particular were targeted for ridicule and rejection.

Once dual tiers of life had been established philosophically and justified theologically, social structures mirroring that kind of thinking followed automatically. Education closed to women; commerce closed to women; government closed to women; theology closed to women; the entire public arena closed to women. Women, men reasoned, and modern philosophers from Hegel to Nietzsche affirmed, were for the comfort of men and the sanctity — read *lineage* — of the family. The rule of the fathers prevailed. Women, patronized as queens of the kitchen, would rule nothing worth ruling or at least nothing for which they themselves were not accountable to men.

The results of such a system have not always been brutal, but they have always been destructive. The patriarchal society, agreeable as it may be, is an essentially violent thing. The patriarchal society — any society in which men, the males of the system, own, administer, shape, or control all the major facets of the culture — is a stifling thing. Not only the intellectual life of a woman is cut off by it, not simply the economic life of a woman is deterred by it, not just the political life of a woman is restricted by it, but the spiritual life of women — and of men, as well — is also corrupted by it. We make ourselves prisoners of a one-sided world. For centuries, women artists, musicians, writers, scientists, and philosophers were excluded from academic life, the public arena, the males-only world stage. We say that women are different from men, and we use those differences to perpetuate society, but we do not engage women in serious ways in order to enrich society.

Patriarchy is more than a set of social structures. It is a cluster of values, a mindset, a way of looking at life, a worldview based on superiority, domination, effectiveness, and conformity. Its effectiveness is not in question. It has consolidated power, raised great monuments, created massive systems, organized whole peoples, girdled the globe, and conquered the world. It has, at the same time, handicapped and corrupted everything it touched, male and female alike. Women had no resources to transform it, and men saw no reason to change it.

Even though some women have profited from the patriarchal system, even as they paid the price of their lives to do it, and even though men have done great good with it as well as evil, patriarchy is essentially wrong, wrong at its roots, and potentially destructive, whatever its effectiveness. The system as system is inadequate.

Patriarchy privileges men, but to talk about patriarchy is not to talk about maleness as such. To be opposed to patriarchy is not to be opposed to men any more than being opposed to communism implies that we should be opposed to Cubans or to any people anywhere who embrace other social-economic philosophies. Patriarchy damages both men and women.

Because of patriarchy, men and women have inherited a truncated notion of God, skewed interpretations of human development, social alienation, and a spiritual wasteland that deprives them both of the right to grow and fail, to fail and grow.

Patriarchy is theologically incongruent. The image of God has become totally male though God in Scripture said it was otherwise. Patriarchy is psychologically unsound. It leads to unbalanced development in both men and women. Patriarchy is socially destructive. It separates the sexes and deprives the world of a total worldview. And, consequently, the spirituality it spawns is deficient. The spirituality promoted by men has been written from the viewpoint of male experience. The theology written by men has been written from the perspective of male questions, male concerns, male priorities, male pressures. What interests men, troubles men, affects men, concerns men has dominated religious thought and practice since the beginning of Christianity. What women know about how and where to experience God has become the stuff of family folklore and local myth, perhaps, but not part of the fabric of the intellectual tradition of the churches.

Patriarchy rests on four interlocking principles: dualism, hierarchy, domination, and essential inequality. These are the touchstones of the patriarchal worldview. These imply, in essence, that reason and feelings are distinct, that the world runs from the top down and that the top is genetically coded, that some humans are more human than other humans and so are in charge of the rest of them, that humans come in two sexes, one of which is fundamentally lesser than the other. Patriarchy takes biological differences, imposes hierarchy on them, gives hierarchy dominative power, and justifies all of it on the theory of intrinsic inequality. But none of it stands to be justified by the life and teachings of Jesus. The Jesus born of a woman without the agency of a man defies in that very generation all the dualism, hierarchy, domination, and inequality practiced in his name.

Modern psychology would certainly debate even the possibility, let alone the value, of trying to divide reason and feeling. Who would argue today that the finest minds are not swayed by feelings or that feelings are not the most humanizing element in the human condition? Albert Einstein, for instance, discovered the principle of an infinitely expanding universe through mathematical formulations long before scientists thought such a thing was possible. Not only did he ignore his calculations; he altered them, in fact, because he himself, a loyal Newtonian, *felt* so strongly that such a conclusion had to be wrong, whatever the rightness of the figures. This great model of rational intelligence for modern society clearly followed his feelings rather than his intellectual calculations. Years later, the astronomer Hubble, using experimental data, confirmed the fact that the universe is indeed expanding, and Hubble, not Einstein, was credited with the discovery. Einstein was appalled. He called it "the biggest blunder of my life." [18] Clearly, feeling and reason intersect, even in the brightest of thinkers. Glorify reason as we will, feelings affect it. The refusal to admit this reality blunts the value of both. Then reason calls itself objective, and feeling calls itself useless, when the truth is that reason is in need of feeling and feeling is in need of respect if human beings are to be human at all.

The truth is that people follow hunches and come to unreasonable conclusions which are nevertheless correct. People let their hearts lead them and make great decisions whatever their lack of detachment from the matter at hand. People become mentally ill or physically sick when their feelings are blocked. To deny reason the benefit of feeling is to presage the worst of human possibilities. It allows for the Holocaust, the bombing of Hiroshima, the ownership of slaves, the extermination of the Indian, and the invisibility of half the human race — women — because at one level all of those were reasonable proposals. The Holocaust, it was argued, would purify the race. The atomic bombing of Hiroshima killed women and children to save soldiers. Slavery brought economic stability to Spain and created a competitive textile industry for the United States. The decimation of Indians enabled the settlement of the West. The disenfranchisement of women provided a service system to sustain the public sector. What kind of spirituality is that? It is a sterile mind, at best, that defines one way of thinking as the only way of thinking and so denies the church, the community, and the society a kind of thinking that looks at facts through feelings.

Patriarchy argues, unconvincingly and illogically, that men are higher human beings than women though women have creative bodies as well as creative minds. It talks about male and female roles, says hierarchy is ordained by God, and then denies women the right to use both their bodies and their minds. Over half the women of the world are illiterate to this day because schooling is denied them because they are female. Over half the minds of this world are denied the right to think. On the other hand, over half the world — men — are denied the creativity, the sensitivity, the intuition, the insight, the intelligence of the other half, as well. It is an inhuman approach to the human condition.

Patriarchy, a system based on biology theologized, divides humanity into two categories and declares one of the categories, because it is different, unequal. Patriarchy ranks and orders everything. Patriarchy sucks power to the top or passes it down in gradually decreasing doses. Patriarchy is built on the backs of the powerless by the powerful, who take all power to themselves, public, intellectual, and religious.

In patriarchal societies, women are minimized, trivialized, made invisible, and shunted to the margins by a system that bases itself on their inferiority. They are also often seduced by a reverence that applauds them but limits them. They are eulogized for staying in their proper places, for being sufficiently docile and properly deferent, but they are also degraded by the false protectionism, veneration, paternalism, and denigration that such a system offers. The patriarchal woman buys her place in such a society at the price of her person. More than that, she limits the development of every other woman as well. In a patriarchal society, females can be children, daughters, girls, "little wives," and mothers but never independent, self-sustaining, totally developed women, adults. In this society, women who want to do what they are able to do are snickered at behind their backs and hooted out of rooms.

There is, however, an aspect of patriarchy that is commonly overlooked in the feminist critique and in the male defense of it as well. Patriarchy, an intellectual scheme based on inequality and control by powerful males, destroys men as well as women. Many men, seduced by the superficial rewards of the society or conditioned into its patterns by a theology of headship, seldom realize what they have given up, both psychologically and spiritually, to gain those rewards.

Men in a patriarchal system are denied personal expression. The boy who cries gets labeled a sissy. Real men take pain, their own and everyone else's, without wincing, without feeling, without responding. They learn to stand in rivers of pain, to defy it, to inflict it, to scoff at it, to create it, and ignore it, and call it strength. The man who cries risks loss of respect. Consequently, a man learns to channel feelings into anger. If he throws things, he's upset. If he shouts at his children, he's had a hard day. If he lapses into sullen silence, he's worrying about something. If he abuses his wife, he's frustrated at work. Legitimate emotions become masked in men and one-dimensional. Men starve for the right to have feelings that don't demean them.

Personal relationships suffer, too. Men are trained to achieve and compete, not to support, not to understand, not to compassionate, not to stand by. They have buddies, not friends. To hide a fear of failure, they learn early to brag about their own exploits, regardless how mundane, and to discredit the efforts of others. Life becomes a series of tests and games and losses in which they never have the right to fail, the chance to be dependent, and the right to grow through all the stages of life with calm and confidence. Life becomes a series of steps on the way to the top and the insistent denial of the inevitable transition into nothingness. Emotional development becomes a lonely, private enterprise. Getting ahead, making money, becoming powerful, having answers, suppressing feelings, and being in charge come to consume them. Life goes into work and power rather than into relationships.

Men learn to expect status, service, and submission. They lose the right to be wrong. They are denied the obligation to learn from others. They use things — money, power, and property — to define themselves. They work till they drop, and they drop from working. They have little emotional release. They lose contact with children who bring the child out in us all and give us purpose for the future and compassion in the present. They detach themselves from feminine things and lose a whole side of themselves to power games and profiteering. They learn to suppress their sense of inadequacy and substitute authority for competency both at work and at home. Men learn to be strong rather than weak, in control rather than dependent. They lose the sense of security that comes from good relationships. Men learn young not to trust women because women, they know, are essentially inferior. They learn, as well, to compete with other men because men are obstacles to their own advancement. They learn to be hard rather than soft. Examples abound: A young man, blond-haired, bright-eyed, and flushed with excitement, climbed out of his plane, fresh from a bombing run over Iraq that strafed thousands of young Iraqis running through the desert for home.

"How was it out there?" a reporter asked him dolefully.

The boy looked straight into the television camera, grinned, and said with gusto, "It was a turkey shoot!"

So much for patriarchal spirituality and its development of the gentle and sensitive man.

As a result of such formation, men lose the wisdom of women, the grace of the feminine, even the intellectual complement of the so-called complementarity arguments. Their social lives become focused on independence, status, efficiency, prestige, and power. Their spiritual lives become focused on ritual and law, institutions and theories, dogmas rather than feelings, law rather than justice. Such a system is a long, long way from Galilee.

What is sad, but not surprising, is the fact that the spirituality which emerges in a patriarchal system reflects, and supports, the system itself. A patriarchal worldview projects onto spirituality the beliefs and values current in patriarchy. If God is male, then men are closer to God than women are. If maleness is more divine than femaleness, then what men want, what men think, what men value, God wants, thinks, values. The fear of displeasing a male father-God becomes the foundation of the spiritual life. Exclusion from sacristy and sanctuary, from hymns and prayers, from language and legislations of those who are not the right gender is taken for granted in a system that prizes a hierarchy of social classes and promotes it theologically. Clericalism, division based on privilege and spiritual rank, makes for standard fare. The church belongs to men. The mind of God belongs to men. The service of God belongs to men. Theology belongs to men — and all its definitions, all its canons, all its dogmas, all its doctrines, and all its judgments. It is a sad, sad substitute for the Jesus who played with little children, sent women to evangelize whole cities, cured lepers on the Sabbath, and called God Daddy, — not Master, not Lord, not Patriarch, not the kind of father the Roman system knew so well — just Daddy, the one who loves. As mothers do.

Jesus, it seems, knew no boundaries. Jesus had brash and brazen things in mind for the human race, stifled later by a spirituality too small for the project. Patriarchy became a lens that filtered out the feminine aspect of Jesus, that obscured the feminine side of God. Surely there is more to God than control and anger, hierarchy and law. As the poet Rumi says, "Out beyond ideas of wrongdoing and right doing there's a field. I'll meet you there." [19]

Now, in a century with eyes wide open to the evils of domination, the sin of exclusiveness, the other humanity of the feminine, a God of infinitely gentle heart waits for all of us outside old systems and old rules at someplace new.

Feminism

THE NEW WORLDVIEW

It happened on July 20, 1969, the night Neil Armstrong landed on the moon. "One small step for man," he said. "One giant leap for mankind." I never even heard the exclusion in the term. Those were the days when the invisible woman either didn't know she was invisible or didn't care that she didn't exist in the real world, that she wasn't counted in the census figures of many nations, that she couldn't borrow money even in the United States, this so-called great democratic model of equality. We — Guadalupe, the visiting Hispanic exchange-program teacher, and I — were out walking up and down in front of the house. I was standing head back to see I-don't-know-what — the American flag, maybe — up there where human beings were at that very moment unfurling it to open a new frontier.

"Well, there it is — our moon," I said, much in the spirit, I'm sure, of the Romans who pronounced the Mediterranean "Mare Nostrum," our sea, and the English who received land grants in the New World and the pioneers who opened the West. I saw her eyebrows rise and felt her tighten her arms against her tiny waist.

"No," she said, in an accent thick with the sound of rolling r's, "it is not your moon. That moon belongs to all of us and always will — and so does this planet." I knew I had said something very, very wrong. It would be years before I understood how really wrong it was. And I am learning yet.

We like to think that we mold ideas. We give very little attention to the degree to which ideas mold us. We give even less attention to how little we question them, how much they justify, how impervious they are to change. Patriarchy taught us all, for instance, men and women alike, of the inevitability of domination. We took as truth that some people were up and some down, that some people had a right to own the moon and that others did not, and that God wanted it that way. God wanted white Western males in charge of things — "the white man's burden" they called it — and defined everyone else as lesser: less intelligent, less worthy, less human. Patriarchy teaches women their invisibility, and women themselves believe the right-ness of it. We live for years and never question the foundations on which our very lives are based, our institutions rest, and our spirituality, the way we live out our faith, depends.

The French philosopher Blaise Pascal wrote three centuries ago what may well be the real effect of thinking. He said, "It is true that force rules the world, but opinion looses force." [20] It is an ominous insight. It rings a clam-orous truth. When the credibility of an idea erodes, the power of the idea disintegrates. Only the skeleton of force remains. Only the ability to restrict continues to operate in institutions in such a system. Its ability to energize, people discover one morning, has been long gone. Then the signs of such change appear everywhere: Public criticism begins; internal dissension erupts; the institution dies from the inside out.

At the same time, such places seldom simply disappear. They stay in place, ghosts of their former selves, sites of some kind of private and pious consolation, perhaps, but for all practical purposes stripped of effect in the public arena. They simply lose their power to influence.

But if that is true, and social history is rife with the bones of once vibrant systems now defunct — monarchies leveled, economic systems felled, religions reduced to the level of quaint custom — then at this very moment there are termites in the foundation of patriarchy. The ideas are in contest. As far as more and more women are concerned, a spiritual tradition based on rejection of the self, invisibility in the system, or inequality in the home has lost its claim to moral purity. And they are saying so.

Religion itself, the great value agent of culture, is being reevaluated for patriarchal distortion of its liberating roots. Some feminists stay in churches for love of the tradition but without respect for the structures. Some women stay in a church but worship with women's groups as well. Many of them have left their churches already, never to be seen again — part of other faiths now or involved with no traditional faith at all. Those who return to the church, if they ever do, come back, in most part, for the sake of their children, for whom they seek a spiritual education but whose catechesis they edit. Parents have become the teachers of spiritual education, and, for a growing number of them — if the array of articles, survey responses, and petitions are to be trusted — that translates as a responsibility to mount a clear and confident contradiction of canons, practices, and moral instructions based on the inferiority of women, the inequality of the sexes, and the invisibility of women in church or society. What's more, they debate such subjects in the presence of their children. They answer questions more out of disquiet than out of heart. "Mama, why are there no girl priests in our church?" the small daughter of a Canadian couple demanded to know one Sunday morning after Mass.

"Because," her parents answered, uncomfortable at having to deal so early with the question they knew would someday be inevitable, "our church doesn't allow girl priests. Yet."

"Then," the little girl asked, astonished, "why do we go there?"

Parents, both mothers and fathers, do not correct attitudes like that anymore. On the contrary, they themselves are cautioning their children against accepting such positions without qualification, without reservation. They are admitting their own discomfort, their own confusion, their own rejection of ideas that defy the liberating message of the gospel. They pronounce such things downright wrong and make a distinction for their children between the faith, the tradition, the gospel, and the institution. They are making clear differentiations between the spiritual values they have been taught in the Jesus tradition and the structures of the churches which purport to embody it. That kind of catechesis builds another spirituality in the shell of the old one.

In the face of such public misgiving, to stem the tide of doubt, letters of condemnation and clarification are pouring out of church bureaucracies. Theologians are being silenced. Bishops are being admonished. Organizations bent on discussion, change, or renewal in the churches are being threatened. People are being condemned. Petitions are being ignored. And nothing changes. The stream of thought in contradiction to official positions on male superiority continues to flow out of journals, books, academic consultations, and popular magazines despite the disapproval, despite all injunctions to the contrary. The people are bent on being heard. It is a new church whether anyone wants it to be new or not. Ideas are running rampant. Why? Because the old ones have been looked at and found wanting by both women and men alike. Why? Because spirituality is being brought to bear on spiritual systems which, captive to patriarchal cultures, preach one set of values and model another. No such questioning, no such emendations, no such thing as doubt, no such independence in the faith life could ever have happened in my childhood.

Women are speaking out everywhere, talking back, speaking up, straightening their shoulders, and responding to the issues despite the fact that they have not been asked the questions. In that sense, then, the church has already been feminized.

What is lacking, of course, is the inclusion of women in the structures of the church itself, not as token clerics, parish helpers, or pious observers, but as members, as authorities, as ministers, as theologians, as spiritual directors, as bishops, as women. Obviously, the dualism still exists. The only difference now is that this time it comes wearing a smiling face. It says, "We're sorry," and then it says, "but we can't help it." It says, "You're human," and then it says, "but a very special kind of human," which, translated, means "not a male human," another kind of human: unique, special, different — too unique, too special, too different to be what was really incarnated, fully baptized, definitely full of grace, or genuinely created in the image of God, regardless of what God had to say about it.

The problem is that fewer and fewer people every day believe such things. Pascal's insight takes on a current color: "It is true that force rules the world, but opinion looses force" becomes more warning than insight. Decline in churchgoing among both women and men of all faiths pinpoints the erosion that even now haunts and torments, stalks and troubles the churches. It bells the cat. It sounds the alarm. It records in cold, clear numbers the slow, slow process that is changing the face of humankind. It is an important vein to follow because it marks a step-over point in history, a cataclysm of changing perspective reminiscent of the Reformation in its immensity. The new awareness seeps like lava through fissures in a rock. It can not be held back. It is the feminization of human consciousness bringing the sensibilities of a feminist spirituality to a grievously patriarchal world and a church seriously suspect in its patriarchal form.

The ideas that have held women in spiritual vassalage as well as in social confinement, that have lulled men into arrogant darkness and bogus omniscience, paint a picture of humanity that does the idea of God no favor. The very thought that one type of human being was made for the pleasure and service of the other makes of God a kind of taunting bully. The notion that God would create women with brains and forbid them to use them paints God as some kind of sadist. The notion that the God of Mary and Eve and of Joseph and Adam, their helpmates, trusts more to men than to women ignores the very place of women in the Christian tradition. The notion that God is a sexist appalls.

And yet, faithful to the male-supremicist thinking of theologians from the time of Augustine and Tertullian, such tenets have been the coin of the modern philosophical realm, the basis of contemporary theological thought in the Western world, never condemned by major church documents, never decried from the pulpits of the Christian world. And why? The answers are too obvious to be ignored, too embarrassingly simple to be repeated. When the center of intellectual life moved out of the monasteries into the universities, whatever contribution women had been able to make to the development of thought through their own schools, came, for all intents and purposes, to a professional if not an abrupt halt. Women were now barred from the university system as well as the synods of the church. Men, always the writers of history, now became its professors. Men, now the professional storytellers, wrote the stories of men. Men made the rules and made rules that benefited men. Men explained the universe. Men interpreted the Scriptures. Men wrote the philosophy texts and enshrined the ideas of male philosophers. Men constructed the theologies that maintained the history of women in the churches. "Women," Thomas Aquinas, archtheologian of the Middle Ages, taught in his definitive compendium of Christian thought, *Summa Theologica,* "are subordinate both in nature and in purpose...." They are, therefore, he reasoned, carnal by nature and "have not sufficient strength of mind to resist concupiscence." [21] Those ideas not only justified the oppression of women; they were also the ideas that, by implication, created a spirituality that limited women and anchored men in notions of preeminence as harmful to the men themselves in one way as they were to women in another.

Revolution happened everywhere in the modern world, but little of it happened for women, and for most women yet today, much is still to be accomplished around the world. [22] According to the Fourth United Nations Conference on Women in Beijing, most of the illiterate of the world are still women, most of the underpaid and unemployed are still women, most of the disenfranchised, the socially invisible, the professionally underrepresented, and the legally denied in every society on earth are still women. [23] For centuries every philosopher maintained the rightness of sexism; every theologian sanctified it. As a result, every institution guards itself against women, their values, and their hopes. The walls fall slowly.

Nietzsche, for all his theorizing about power and individual moral choice, maintained the notion to the edge of the twentieth century that women were inherently subordinates. "Women want to serve and find their happiness in this," he said. Rousseau agreed: Women, he wrote, are "fitted by nature to please and be subjected." [24] The function of law, Kant argued, is to assert "the natural superiority of the husband over the wife." [25] "If a union is to be harmonious and indissoluble," he wrote, "it is not enough for two people to associate as they please; one party must be subject to the other." [26] The right to economic independence would "corrupt the morals of the woman," [27] Adam Smith argued. Hegel identified the interests of women with the interest of the family, disregarding completely that women might have ideas and interests of their own. The price of the suppression occurred to him, however. He wrote, "The [community] creates for itself in what it suppresses and what is at the same time essential to it an internal enemy — womankind in general." [28] Clearly, in his mind — and in the minds of theorists after him — the male pattern of society and life took precedence, whatever the cost to women. "Women are capable of education," he wrote, "but they are not made for the activities which demand a universal faculty, such as the more advanced sciences, philosophy, and certain forms of artistic production. Women may have happy ideas, taste, and elegance, but they can not attain to the ideal." [29] Biological differences must, these thinkers insisted, generate social differences.

Teachers, jurists, lawgivers, and theologians absorbed and repeated the teachings of Rousseau that women were less intellectual than men and "their reason not so strong," that they were made to please men, to obey them, and "to put up even with injustice from [them]." [30] In the patriarchal society, a society based on hierarchy and domination, the virtues left to women were obedience and chastity, subservience and fidelity, geared to maintain "the honor of the man."

Change and development, self-improvement and achievement, influence and fame were reserved for men. Women were excluded from public life, from politics, from history, and from full human development. Inferior in essence, they occupied an inferior status in the social schema.

These are the concepts from which modern society, contemporary spirituality, and current social values derive, whatever the talk about "liberty and justice for all." Ideas like these make it very clear why police departments doubted the veracity of raped women, why courts did not indict for domestic violence, why ministers asked women what they were wearing when they were attacked. The implications were clear.

Feminism, a different cluster of values, a distinct worldview, comes to correct patriarchy's skewed concepts of who should be rulers and who should be ruled, who are strong and who are weak, what is right and what is wrong, what constitutes manliness and what defines a woman. Feminism does not come to destroy men. If anything, it comes to save men from imprisonment by a system that cramps the human development of men all the while it purports to give them power. Feminists come to save women in their holy pursuit for equality from adopting the patriarchal style of the system to which they aspire. Feminists are not asking men to be less than manly. Feminists are asking women and men not to buy into patriarchal systems that destroy them both. Feminism comes to bring both men and women to the fullness of life, the wholeness of soul, for which we were all made in the image and likeness of God.

Men become pawns of the power structure in a patriarchal system. Women become invisible. To be subsumed, subservient, and derivative requires a theology of diminishment that Jesus denied in his association with women. Jesus treated women as full adults, discussed deep theological questions with them, and raised them from the dead. Mary of Nazareth, like Eve, had the right to free choice in life. The angel Gabriel, Scripture says, asked Mary a question which she had full right to answer one way or another, freely. The first person to whom Jesus described himself as Messiah was a woman, a Samaritan woman, an outcast. The only corpse Jesus touched in Scripture, an act which according to the law rendered him unclean, was the corpse of the daughter of Jairus. Independence, equality, and autonomy shine in those relationships, and it is independence, equality, and autonomy that feminists pursue for all the oppressed of the world. The point is this: The gospels provide a model of male-female relationships that few churches, if any, have fully modeled since the time of Jesus. Feminist spirituality is a call to live the gospel, not the prevailing culture.

Feminism emerges out of the growing consciousness that the lives of women, and the social order in general, center on sometimes subtle but always systematic oppression designed to use one half of humanity for the service of the other. Feminist spirituality derives from the conviction that the liberation Jesus came to bring to this world is yet unaccomplished and that Christianity, captured by culture, is oftentimes more patriarchal than Christian, whatever its best intents and better teachings.

Like patriarchy, feminism, too, is a worldview, a way of relating to the rest of the world, a consciousness of the equality of differences. The difference between patriarchy and feminism is that feminism looks at life from the other side, the underside, the forgotten side. Feminism critiques cultures built on power for some and powerlessness for many. Feminism makes us ask what it would take to build societies in which some people were not written out of the public arena before they ever had a chance to get into it in the first place. When we seek the right to quit the power game, to render the face of humanity to include the excluded, to realize that no one part of us is the norm for all of us, feminism becomes a reality.

Feminism requires us to stop thinking in ladders. To the feminist, people are not up or down, disposable or valuable, higher or lower than others. We are all simply dignified parts of the human enterprise, each of us making a critical contribution to a common goal, the development of humankind. When women claim their right to have their experiences heard and responded to, feminism frees everyone to think broader thoughts. When minorities refuse to be silent, feminism flowers. When respect for one another replaces both unfounded rejection and unlimited reverence, feminism expresses the fact of interdependence. When majorities anywhere — the poor, the indigenous, the disenfranchised, the laity, the women — refuse to be tools of a powerful minority, Christianity emerges in feminist form.

Feminism sees otherness as a way to enrich a society. Conference tables, synods, parliaments, and bank boards that are all old, all white, all male, and all middle class may have power, but they lack perspective. They lack a sense of what they do not know. They assume unto themselves the wisdom that comes from universal experience, but they have not had it, and they do not include it in their deliberations. They name themselves "the universal subject," the ones with the right to speak for everyone else without even asking the rest of the world if that's all right. When disenfranchised groups refuse to be subsumed in the dominant society, feminism begins to change the world.

Feminism assumes the inherent equality, the essential value of the other. The feminist assumes an independent other, the one who is free to be interdependent rather than defined into dependence. To the feminist everyone and everything has rights. Poor people are not here to be exploited by rich people for slave wages. Women are not here to be the play toys of men. Wives are not here to be the servants of husbands. Men are not here to be discarded in their prime by a corporate world so that more profit can seep to the top, thanks to the exploitation of the people at the bottom. Animals are not here to be disposed of for idle sport. The globe is not here to be wrung dry by the people with enough guns, enough money, enough power to rape the rainforests and colonize the moon. People are not here to stack the socioeconomic pyramid so that people at the top can stand on the backs of those on the bottom.

The feminist knows that all of us need one another, that no one has all the answers, the fullness of revelation, the whole of wisdom, the last insight, the whole of holiness. The piece of life that each of us brings to the adventure of life is guide and gift to the rest of us. Feminist spirituality follows the Jesus who sought out tax collectors and zealots, women and children, Pharisees and paralytics pronounced to be in sin and raised them all to the height of his own soul.

Respect for otherness, equality, mutuality, interdependence, and nurturance are basic components of a feminist worldview. That kind of thinking necessarily changes the configuration of the human community from a pyramid to a circle.

There is no doubt: A feminist spirituality would change marriage, change society, change church, change the very definition of sanctity. Feminist values touch the core of Christianity as we know it. They call us to the Christianity of the Jesus who preceded the patriarchal church. They call us to listen to the Canaanites in our midst, to include women in our groups, to do away with rigid roles, to see ourselves as part of the whole rather than its leaders, to go through life as partners rather than power mongers, to devote ourselves to more than ourselves. Those concepts would change domestic legislation and foreign policy, theology and corporate life, families and churches. Those concepts would turn the world upside down. They are holy-making ideas for our time. No wonder they threaten the system so much.

CHRISTIANITY AND FEMINISM

A MIRROR IMAGE

The old bishop sat deep in the large leather chair, his wide forehead lined with furrows that came together in a tight knot over his thick eyebrows. I liked the man. He was honest and thoughtful and very, very sincere. We were into one of those tight, dense conversations about what the church wanted of women and what the diocese would allow in liturgy. "I certainly want the parishes to include women wherever they can," he said, "but we have a basic disagreement, you and I, about all of this feminist talk. I tell you, Joan, feminism has wreaked untold amounts of damage on marriage and the family."

"Bishop," I said, "we don't disagree on ideas. We disagree on the punctuation marks. The problem is that you use a period where I would use a semicolon."

"And what does that mean?" he said.

"Well, Bishop," I said, "I would have agreed with you if you had said the whole sentence. Yes, it is certainly true that feminism is changing marriage as we knew it — semicolon — but that's because patriarchy has been wreaking untold amounts of damage on marriage for centuries."

His eyebrows went up, froze a moment, and then, a little wanly, he smiled. Hope rose in me for one more time, lank and slight perhaps, but real.

The question rises repeatedly: Is it possible for a person to be a good feminist and a good Christian at the same time? The answer is: How is it possible to be a good Christian without being a good feminist? For Christians, when the two become separated, they are both the worse for it. One requires the other. One reflects the other. Neither of them stands well alone.

Feminism without spirituality runs the risk of becoming what it rejects: an elitist ideology, arrogant, superficial, and separatist, closed to everything but itself. Without a spiritual base that obligates it beyond itself, calls it out of itself for the sake of others, a pedagogical feminism turned in on itself can become just one more intellectual ghetto that the world doesn't notice and doesn't need. Elitism in any society puts distance between the literati and those defined as not quite as worthy, not quite as knowledgeable, not quite as sophisticated as they. The literati are those in any society who hold a secret among themselves and look down on those who do not know the secret these intelligentsia will not tell them. If women have felt anything uncomfortable in feminism in the last twenty years, it has often been a sense of rejection by certain elements of the women's movement itself, by those women who are as rigid in their definitions of women as patriarchy had been before them.

The situation is more complex than it seems. Intent on gaining the right to function as capable and contributing individuals, not simply as groups of wives and mothers, second-wave feminists — the Betty Friedan, Gloria Steinem, Adrienne Rich generation — took up the failed suffragette ideals of first-wave feminists that had collapsed in the romantic notion that the vote itself would create a new world for women. In the end, they broke great ground for both women and men but broke it often at the cost of the primary values of feminism itself. In no position to negotiate, they made demands. Unable to lead balanced lives, they demanded new ones instead of balanced ones. Unrepresented, unheard, and unwanted anywhere in the public arena, in order to be reckoned with, they made necessary spectacles of themselves everywhere, just as their grandmothers before them had done to gain the vote. Many women who wanted both a family life and a public life rather than one or the other — what the men in their lives took for granted, incidentally — felt left out of the process of feminist emancipation. Many men, sensing something wrong with the patriarchal worldview and something right about a feminist perspective, reached out to identify with feminism themselves and felt the exclusion with a vengeance. The movement ran ahead of the pack and, in some cases, became a classic case of elitism. Other feminisms arose to right the imbalance or the theoretical directions. But the spiritual question remains. Unyielding postures are understandable in the light of history but less than true to feminism itself. If left unaddressed spiritually, the results of such zeal can be destructive of women, of men, and of the movement itself. Elitism is always and everywhere a scourge to its own best ideals.

The elite hold themselves above those who have not had the same experiences as they. They avoid those who do not have the same insights. They derogate those who do not have the same goals for whatever the movement whose banner they carry. They become more ideological than idealistic. For elitists, in their best-of-all-possible worlds, there is a true feminism and a naive one. There is a real feminist and a bogus one. There are orthodox feminists and those who flirt with the enemy. To those who are feminist purists, there is no such thing as a feminist man and no such thing as a full-time mother who is also a real feminist. Too easily, the oppressed become the oppressors, not because they seek to, perhaps, but because that is the style most familiar to them in the patriarchal society that taught them how to oppress. It is so easy to become harsh with people who have not seen what we have seen. The feminist, like the elite of any endeavor, in other words, struggles with the tension between theory and vision, between the doctrinaire and the spiritual.

The healthy feminist needs the spiritual dimension of life in a very special way. The road to new consciousness is not only a long one. It is a lonely one as well. Without a spiritual vision as well as a social one, the various injunctions of the spiritual life — to love one another, to hate the sin but love the sinner, to treat others the way we want to be treated — too easily collapse under the noonday sun of slow-moving structures and closed-minded people. Then acrimony sets in; then the feminism that takes the world to its heart goes the way of mythology and fairy tales, an ideal to be espoused but not to be expected.

When the group itself, the feminist enclave, becomes more the place to be — away from the dust and grime of change — than in the midst of the human community, where feminist values and concerns are most in need of modeling, feminism ceases to be effective, ceases to be Christian. It is Christian spirituality that leaves us open to Canaanite and Samaritan, to Pharisee and leper. If feminism becomes perceived as a cult, a collection of those who have exclusive knowledge of a higher life, it will soon be that but nothing else. Then the hope to leaven society ends with the marginalization of the very people able to prod it to see itself differently.

Those involved in social change, and feminists are no exception, who lose touch with spirituality tend to turn what should be valorous acts of the highest level of human community into the temporary, the political, the mundane. They burn out from lack of perspective. Eventually, infinitesimally small gains made in the face of eons of systemic wrong take their toll. With limited inner strength to fall back on, they wilt in the face of loss after loss. And in the course of the strain, feminists without spirituality become dry and tired. Then, discouragement turns to bitterness and energy fails. Then, what is important becomes what is impossible. The soul shrivels, and the heart fails. Going on becomes more effort than even a zealot can muster.

We get tired. We get discouraged. We start to quit. Then the temptation is to make feminism more a refuge from reality, a nest to hide in, than a reality to be accomplished. The fact is that we do not do feminism to succeed; we do feminism because we can not morally do otherwise.

For casting a ballot with fifteen other women in 1872, Susan B. Anthony was arrested in New York, tried, and fined a hundred dollars. She refused to pay the fine even though threatened with jail. Driven by hope, she started her campaign all over again, but it took fifty more years before the United States government granted women the right to vote. Massive social change comes slowly and silently, in imperceptible ways and in God's good time, not ours. We take for granted now what Susan B. Anthony gave her life to gain, but without the courage to do the same, we will leave nothing behind for the next generation from our own struggles. That kind of commitment takes deep faith, enduring hope, and the fortitude of martyrs. [31]

Separatist feminists seek to create a society within a society. They cut themselves off from the world around them. In the short term, the strategy may provide some psychological relief and necessary respite from the pressure of trying to bring an entire society to see life from another perspective. Nevertheless, separating people into categories, dividing things into groups, polarizing concepts into opposites makes anything very easy to isolate, very easy to ignore. It is precisely what Jesus set out to avoid by refusing to be a military messiah, by paying Roman taxes, by keeping the high holy days, all the while curing paralytics on the Sabbath and overturning tables in the temple.

Frustrated by a society that bars women as a matter of principle from serious public participation, separatist feminists make men as a class the enemy. Then, shut in by the impermeable boundaries around them, isolationism freezes them into place. At least unwittingly, for the sake of providing for themselves a world without challenge, a world without struggle, they abandon the feminist commitment to bring people together. They belie the principles espoused by feminism itself by alienating one group from another.

Separation is not cured by separation. "Good fences" may, indeed, "make good neighbors," as the character in the Robert Frost poem "Mending Wall" remarks, but only if the forces on each side of the line meet there as equals. As it is, we have had barriers enough. We need feminists now who stay in the conversation, never giving an inch to repression, who never flinch in the face of rejection, who never fail to speak out for the rights of women, who never fail to assume, to expect, to claim equal partnership in the project of being human. At the same time, the Christian feminist knows that one of the principles of feminism is to step over boundaries, to reach out, to listen, and to demand respect and dignity in the process. Feminism does not set out to create boundaries. Only a solid spiritual life provides the depth and the strength that stepping over traces and dealing with otherness demands. We need the faith to know that what God created in two sexes, in multiple colors, and in various parts of the globe all own the moon.

With little or no spiritual base to draw upon, the feminist, facing sexism everywhere — at work, in the home, and, perhaps most discouragingly of all, in the church — faces a long, hard struggle to distinguish between the patriarchal system and maleness itself.

Whatever the ideals, the struggles to achieve them for both men and women are at base deeply human. Feminist men report multiple reactions in the course of their own coming to consciousness. Some feel shame about being a man. Some suffer embarrassment when they're with women's groups. Some experience a kind of self-loathing when they are with macho men. Being a man ceases to be a good thing for them.

Women struggle, too. Feminist women with little or no spiritual base can find themselves responding negatively to men in general. Many begin to see sexism everywhere, and, like the fox under the toga in the children's story, it eats away at their innards, destroying relationships and fueling deep and lasting anger. The awareness that both men and women have been affected, crippled, by the values, structures, and goals of patriarchy fades, and life becomes more a battle of the sexes, a souring of the soul, than a stretching of human horizons.

Finally, feminists without spirituality ignore the effect of spirituality on the mindset of the rest of the world. Structural change is not enough. The achievement of equal pay for women, professional promotions, child care, and the calculation of domestic wages in the GNP will do nothing for the relative worth of women if theology and philosophy continue to be based on ancient assumptions about woman's essential inferiority, natural weakness, or special nature. In fact, we have seen the proof of that already. Women got the vote, but, at the level of social philosophy, nothing changed. Women got education, but nothing changed. Women got jobs, but nothing changed. Women were still defined, ranked, treated as second-class. Some structures changed, yes, but underneath it all, sexism and patriarchy remained rooted in the culture. Institutions simply adjusted to new kinds of sexism. Only the structures on the lowest of levels changed; attitudes and unspoken understandings about the ladder of hierarchy and pyramids of power remained in place. People knew, despite a few minor social adjustments here and there, who was meant, in the end, to remain on top, whatever the abilities and giftedness of the people on the bottom. The task of feminism today lies in changing the assumptions upon which exclusion, hierarchy, domination, and sexism rest. It lies in rediscovering the feminist strain in Christianity and reclaiming it for a world gone mad with patriarchy.

A commitment to change the mindset of the world, its values and its structures, from patriarchy to feminism is no small task, and yet, unless we do it — and soon — there may be no world worth saving at all.

The prospect of feminism without spirituality is a dour one. But the prospect of spirituality without feminism is even worse, I think. Feminism without spirituality is fragile, but spirituality without feminism is incomplete at best, sterile at its worst. Spirituality without feminism is simply a vehicle for patriarchy. It maintains what it preaches against. It preaches universal love and respect and maintains sexist or exclusive language in its hymns. It preaches a new equality and universal human value and keeps women off altars just as the Pharisees kept women from the Holy of Holies. It preaches the Jesus who talked with women in a culture that forbade the public mixing of the sexes and itself practices an Aristotelian philosophy of exclusion. It says one thing and structures another. It defines women by their biology and men by their minds. It fixes life more by maleness than by humanness.

Until the way women read Scripture is as valid a reading of Scripture as the way men read it, the church stands to die from a paucity of ideas. It is not enough to have women with degrees in theology. We must have female theologians at the very center of the development of theological ideas. Women theologians must teach in seminaries, preach in pulpits, translate the texts, and write the documents that become known as the documents of the church. Women must bring to bear on the Christian tradition a woman's understanding of Mary at Pentecost; a woman's commentary on Hagar, the abandoned woman; a woman's interpretation of Eve, the mother of humankind.

Spirituality without feminism will lose even more of the next generation of women than it has of this one. While publishers and businesses and governments make changes to include women and level hierarchies and change structures and mirror the concerns and population of a changing world at all levels, churches continue to insist that God does not want women, does not want change in the one place that counts, the center of the church. Who will stay in a church like that? Who will believe in a God like that?

Where will Christian feminists go for spiritual nourishment if the church itself fails to reflect the feminism of Jesus? If tradition becomes a reason for churches, for synagogues, for mosques to refuse to change in the light of new insights and understandings, on what grounds can we expect change from other institutions? Is the argument from tradition enough to maintain the institution of slavery? Is the argument from tradition sufficient to justify the division between the churches? Is the ecumenical movement — which popes, patriarchs, and theologians are now working so hard to achieve — defunct because separation is more traditional than unity? Where will any sincere Christian go for spiritual direction if tradition is more important to the church than ongoing revelation is? If the awareness of God in the past is more profound, more illuminating, than the awareness of God in the present, what can possibly be the hope for a world on the verge of a universe it never imagined in its theology?

Over the centuries, the Israelites moved from the concept of God as warrior to the idea of God as wisdom, from the notion of a tribal God to a universal God who did not belong to Israel despite Israel's mission to witness to the God who is one. Throughout time, Christianity, too, has grown in its awareness of who Jesus is and what of the mind of God Jesus came to reveal by consorting with Romans and Samaritans, with Canaanites and tax collectors, with Pharisees and women. To close off the possibility of new insights into the mind of God now is to close this generation off to the Holy Spirit. Can there be a greater religious sin?

Patriarchy is the social system in which the church took root. It is Roman in origin, legal in concept, and pre-Christian at its philosophical roots. It is not in itself a revelation. Patriarchy and Christianity are not synonyms. One can certainly exist without the other and does. In fact, to be Christian is to be called to reject anything that excludes the other, that diminishes the other, that denies the other the fullness of life, that uses the other for its own gratification and profit. Any spirituality that justifies oppression, invisibility, domination, and exploitation mocks the very essence of Christianity.

To talk about the damage done to patriarchal institutions by feminism and not to recognize the damage done by patriarchy to those same institutions, to both women and men, to the entire Christian dispensation, cries to heaven for justice, for mercy, for conversion.

The breakthrough has come. We see differently now. We see women as full adults, as total human beings, as individual persons who can not, may not, be subsumed under maleness, who must be dealt with directly, individually, and equally, who must be included, who must be named more than "the little wife" or "the girls." A world listing badly to the side of maleness must begin to honor feminist perceptions, to respect feminist perspectives, to value feminist values before patriarchy saps the soul out of all of us. A spirituality that is not feminist today can not lay claim to being a spirituality at all.

But what does that mean and how would life look if we ever did it?

REASON AND FEELING

A NEW WAY OF THINKING

The small parish high school in which I was teaching at the time had been operated and staffed by an order of nuns for over a hundred years. It had a reputation as one of the best schools in the diocese, in fact. Over 90 percent of its students went to college; almost all of them stayed there to graduate. Nuns had been drilling good work habits, basic skills, quality performance into the children of the small, poor area for years. When the parish school closed to make room for a central high school, however, the diocese appointed a headmaster rather than a sister-principal. What was the difference, I wondered? I soon found out.

One of the first acts of the new headmaster was to name a male disciplinarian and create by his own fiat a demerit system remarkable for its precision. It required quite clearly, for instance, three demerits for chewing gum, five demerits for talking in the hall, six demerits for failing to hand in homework. For a given number of demerits, a student would be suspended, even expelled. "Whew," I thought, "we never did anything like this before. Things are going to be tough around here from now on."

The demerit system was a masterpiece of behavioral objectives before the term even existed in most schools, let alone the process. It was also, it seemed, a simple if harsh method. Cut and dried. If this, then that. What could possibly go wrong in such a system? I discovered the answer the hard way. It taught me more about patriarchal philosophy than I ever wanted to know.

Every Friday night, I noticed, the new headmaster stood at the end of the office counter going through demerit slips teachers had handed in during the week. The names of offenders would be posted on the high-school bulletin board the following Monday to warn students of their prox-

imity to the ultimate correction. Some of the slips I watched him check off and put aside; on others papers he seemed to be writing something.

"What do you write on those?" I asked him, curious about what he could possibly be doing to a process that was, for all practical purposes, it would seem, purely automatic.

"Oh," he said, "I have to change some of them. The sisters are inclined to give too many demerits. You know how women are," he said. "So emotional."

Whether he knew it or not, he was doing more to change my mind-set than he was to alter the forms.

When poets talk about the human soul, they do not talk about reason; they talk about feeling. The totally human human being, they enable us to see, is the one who weeps over evil, revels in goodness, loves outrageously, and carries the pain of the world in healing hands. Feeling is the mark of saints. It is Vincent de Paul tending the poor on the back streets of France, Mother Teresa with a dying beggar in her arms, Florence Nightingale tending the wounded in the midst of battle, John the apostle resting trustingly on the breast of Jesus, Damian binding the running sores of lepers on the island of Molokai, the soup-kitchen people in our own towns giving hours of their lives, week after fruitless week, to feed the undernourished children, the homeless women, and the down-and-outs of both the U.S. and Canada, among the richest countries on earth. Feeling, we know deep within us, signals the real measure of a soul.

Without feeling, living becomes one long bland journey to nowhere that tastes of nothing. Take feeling away, and we take away life. Feeling warns of our excesses and alerts us to possibilities. It attaches us and opens us and warns us of danger. Because of our feelings we are able to persevere through hard times and find our way to good times. Feelings lead us to the people who love us through life and satisfy our souls when nothing else about a situation can sustain us at all. Feelings, devoid of thought, made only of mist, become the inner lights that lead us out of harm's way and home to our better selves. Feeling leads us to love the God we can not see and to see the God around us whom we have yet to come to love. To talk about a spiritual life without feeling, to talk about any life at all without feeling, turns the soul to dust and reduces spirituality to the most sterile of initiatives. And yet we do.

The theologian Clement of Alexandria, drawing on the philosophy of the Greek Stoics and the works of Plato, stressed *apatheia*, the destruction of the four main emotions (anger, desire, fear, and pleasure), as an essential element of the spiritual life. [32] Reason became the reigning grace and feeling a bastard child, proper only to the weak and to women. Being emotional became a curse instead of a virtue. Twenty-two of twenty-nine synonyms given for *emotional* in the WordPerfect thesaurus are blatantly negative, ranging from "agitated" to "unstable." To be emotional is the unforgivable sin in a world where only negative sentiment — anger, violence, and vindication — is valiant.

Men eschewed emotion; women depreciated it. Emotion became the cardinal difference between men and women, the standard of excellence that distinguished one from the other. Men were reasonable. Women were "so emotional." Today, consequently, emotion is the missing attribute in human governance and spiritual development alike. It is precisely what both government and spirituality lack, what each of them needs.

Men correct women all the time. They correct their ideas; they correct their interpretations; they correct their feelings. Especially their feelings. Feelings, men have decided, are the basic blight of women. The implications are clear: Lacking high intelligence (read *male* intelligence), women face life forced to rely on emotion to guide them through its complexities. Reason, on the other hand, men have defined as the purview of men. Philosophers as ancient as Plato and as modern as Kant, theologians as early as Tertullian, college texts as recent as the last half of the twentieth century, [33] and popular psychology books on the shelves at the present time all cite feelings as the bane of women and reason as the boon of men. Science since the time of Bacon has glorified reason and the experimental method as the only adequate approach to anything. Here, the philosophers of the Enlightenment insisted, lies truth.

Clearly, men knew things; women only felt things. On the basis of these same assumptions, even childbearing, its place and process, surely an unarguably female arena, became the province of male scientists rather than of women themselves. Given their natural purpose and resulting intellectual handicap, the argument goes, women need men to be their "head." Literally. The argument persists, but the argument lacks substance.

In the first place, experience now establishes that women are as bright as men, even brighter in many ways, if educational data and scholastic achievement count for anything reasonable. [34] In the second place, now that, in some areas of the world, at least, women are being admitted to previously male occupations and male enclaves, performance records show women to be equal to men and often superior. In the light of such extensive experience, the argument that reason is a justification for patriarchal control, patriarchal spirituality, loses its power to persuade. The biological arguments about essential and wide-ranging intellectual differences between the sexes pale, and embarrassingly so.

But that's not the only thing that's wrong with the argument from reason. Reason has some inherent limitations. Reason is simply one way of looking at issues, and a limited one at that. The "reasonable" scientific approach, in fact, works a great deal better with moon rocks than it does with relationships. The wild card in the human, according to Kant, is choice. [35] Responses not limited by the nature of a thing are simply not predictable. However rational our calculations, we still can not predict human behavior with total accuracy. Consequently, the problem with reason is that it is certainly no better than a guess on anything but quantifiable, measurable material, and even there witness the practice of science constantly to subject data to frequent reinterpretation and revision. Where people are involved, reason as we might, there is simply no way to guarantee that what we think might happen actually will happen. Reason is an unreasonable tool.

In situations that require insight, wisdom, and concern to resolve them as well as hard, cold information, feelings bring an invaluable dimension. Feelings are the other kind of intelligence, the alternate kind of knowing, the humane kind of human reasoning.

When we distance thought from feeling, anything is possible. People turn into automatons when feeling is subtracted from the human equation. When feelings do not count, Hiroshima and Nagasaki, the wholesale destruction of civilians in order to save soldiers, become inevitable, necessary, ethical. When feelings are not part of the decision-making process, Auschwitz becomes a challenge to logistics, a problem of what to do with the bodies, rather than a disease of the human mind, the corruption of the human soul that feeling people know it to be. In those cases, a judgment based on details alone lacks an essential part of the data, the most human part of all, perhaps.

We can be seduced by the glorification of reason into thinking that we have really examined an issue fully. We can use reason to hide the emotional cost of decisions that make one kind of sense but lack another. It may, for instance, make economic sense to close a small school in a poor neighborhood, but it may not make social sense in years to come when the children from that school, lost in the maelstrom of the supersystem to which they are bussed, drop out of school to get away from failure and live out the rest of their lives without the skills they need to find jobs, to raise families, to pay taxes. It may make electoral sense to cut welfare for the poor and maintain corporate welfare for the rich, but when poverty becomes destitution in North America, when the cities go to straw from the center out, what will reason have accomplished?

What the world needs may well be less detached intellectualism and more thinking hearts, less law and more compassion. Reason that is not informed by emotion is a dry and sterile thing. It comes up with answers too flawed to be humane, too disjunctive to be moral. Reason can be a very dishonorable approach to the task of being human. The kind of thinking that invented slavery trivialized feeling. The kind of thinking that trivialized feeling invented slavery. The world that developed nuclear bombs and made defense impossible, made fun of the peace movement for eroding national defenses. With the subjective obscured, objectivity too easily becomes hardheartedness. As Alice in Wonderland noted, in such a world "down is up and up is down."

If women have been forbidden the right to reason, men have been diminished by clinging to it blindly. Women, after all, went on thinking, despite the fact that men decreed it impossible for them. Women wrote poetry they could not publish, painted pictures no one would hang, discovered comets no academies would certify. [36] Men, on the other hand, were not allowed to feel, became afraid to feel. Men who admitted to feelings found themselves declared spineless, recreant, cowardly. Or worse. Fathers worked hard to toughen up their sons, to take the woman out of them, to make them manly. With the manliness, unfortunately, came a hardness, an insensitivity, a patina of toughness that proved its ability to endure pain by being willing to inflict pain on others. Men learned to suppress their feelings and opted for alcoholism and heart attacks instead. Anger, the only emotion allowed a man, became the answer to everything and an instrument of control. Men threw things when they hurt, fought when they were humiliated, went into rages to intimidate their families. At the same time, men suffered dearly for the loss of emotion — from depressions that had no name, physical illnesses that had no physical explanation, social relationships that broke down. They numbed themselves to the center of their souls, lost touch with their own feelings, and lost the ability to communicate the things they needed to communicate most. They cauterized their hearts and called the suffering virtue.

The worship of reason, long the theme of philosophers and theologians in the West, surged in the sixteenth century and dominated the intellectual scene for almost two hundred years. At a time of bewildering change and astounding human progress, understanding of the human condition and methods of coping with it began to depart from older models and values. The shift was away from personal relationships to systems and data. Faced with the growth of cities and the social pressures those implied, questions of governance and social order arose to dominate European thinking. The new middle class, created by the burgeoning capitalistic economy, emerged to take its place among the landed gentry and hereditary nobles. New hierarchies flourished on the basis of wealth alone. New inventions touted what seemed to be unlimited possibilities in the human condition. The invention of the printing press made for rapid response to immediate situations. The new scientific method of observation and experimentation, which replaced the more slow-moving and discursive philosophical speculation of the past, ushered in a new kind of knowledge, a promise of certainty more in the hands of scientists than of theologians. The discovery of new worlds led people to question the very definition of humanity. Human beings in general, not just women, now came to be seen as having grades of development, some more human than others. Finally, the religious revolt against longstanding unscientific dogmas and the claim to theocratic authoritarianism snapped the last link between the old world and the new. And through it all, universities were closed to women. [37] There was no way to soften the mix, little with which to challenge the assumptions, no alternative perspectives or experiences to consider. Reason reigned supreme and did it unreasonably well.

The results were as brutal as they were extraordinarily productive. Slavery, the exploitation of the new laboring class, the extermination of whole races of people, and obscene wealth in the midst of dehumanizing poverty marked a society fueled by commitment to scientific detail. And the perceptible data said that wealth was good, that the only thing better than a little wealth was more wealth, that God blessed those who worked hard, that physical differences signaled intellectual, moral, and social differences, that Aristotle was right when he pronounced that "all women and most men were meant to be slaves." There were clearly higher classes and lower classes, and white Western males were the highest class of all. People went to church on one day a week and lived the lives of slave masters and slaves for the rest of the week. Spirituality had become a very private thing. Devotion flourished, but a concept of the God of justice vanished in its wake.

The desensitization of a culture is a terrible thing. Human sacrifice has long been a mark of it. The patriarchal system sacrificed both women and men on the altar of misguided reason and called it God's will. Feminism is not the first movement to critique it. Late-eighteenth-century romanticism saw the dangers of reason run amuck and went to exactly the opposite extreme. Romanticists rejected the Enlightenment emphasis on reason with a passion. They exalted intuition, feeling, inspiration, and the self. Individual rights and the supremacy of the individual took center stage. Nature itself occupied their attention and became their font of wisdom and light. The search for utopia raged. Self became the god of choice, and with it all sense of common values and the general good became secondary or, at very least, paled into insignificance. At its extreme, romanticism became nihilism with its "nothing counts, nothing matters, nothing exists but my experience" philosophy, which led to the abandonment of all external criteria, left the world without a sense of meaning, without a consciousness of purpose, without belief in anything beyond the perceptible. The romanticists had replaced blind belief in the supremacy of reason with belief in nothing at all.

The spiritual response to the heresy of male reason is clearly not romanticism. The spiritual response to the glorification of reason is the Jesus whose feelings were always part of his behavior. The spiritual response to reason unlimited and romanticism unrestrained is the Jesus who mourned the death of his friend Lazarus, had compassion on the crowds, wept over Jerusalem, overturned the moneychangers' tables in the temple, struggled with loneliness in Gethsemane, and felt abandoned on the cross. The answer to reason and romanticism is a feminist spirituality that honors feelings as a necessary component of thought, a witness to care, and a compelling constituent of holiness.

Now, in another period of rapid change, our own era, at the brink of millennium, is looking again at the idols it has made. Force has not worked. The world is alive with refugee populations it can not absorb. Weaponry has lost the power to be effective without totally destroying the globe over temporary political tensions. Science has developed more questions than answers, more doubt than certainty, less security than ferment.

Like the sixteenth century before it, this century is a change point in history. Every institution in this society, every once unassailable idea, is being exposed to scrutiny and reappraisal. Marriage is in a state of flux. Gender roles are changing. Educational theories are in contradiction. Economic concepts are in serious contest. The social order is in upheaval. Governments are under attack. The very meanings of *life* and *death* are changing. The Age of Reason has run its course. Romanticism has left us moral orphans. We need an age of feeling now. We have had all we can bear of patriarchy and its devotion to reason as the ultimate arbiter of humanity. For the sake of the soul of the society, we need feminist spirituality, feminine wisdom, now.

Modern psychology attests to what happens to people whose feelings are repressed. [38] Qualities of life suppressed in one area eventually erupt in another or lie stunted within us, beyond retrieval, beyond their ability to resource our dried-out souls. Laughter that is not released turns too often to sarcasm. Joy that never gets expressed becomes isolating. Fear that is never honored turns quickly to distrust. Sorrow minimized becomes spiritual deafness until, eventually, "principle" devoid of feeling for the effects of an action is no principle at all.

Feminism frees us, requires us, to look feelingly at the consequences reason spawns. It refuses to diminish what emotion spurs us to face. It opens us up to deal with the human cost of intellectual legerdemain. It enables us to hear the muffled squeals of people caught in the cog of the social machine, to speak for them as Jesus spoke for us, to lay down our lives for them as Jesus did for us, to live for something larger than ourselves. A suffering world waits for the release of the feminine at the highest levels of power. Until feeling becomes a sign of strength rather than a mark of weakness, that can never happen.

Feeling welcomes us to the human race, where, in the end, the fullness of humanity is all any of us will have to show for being spiritual.

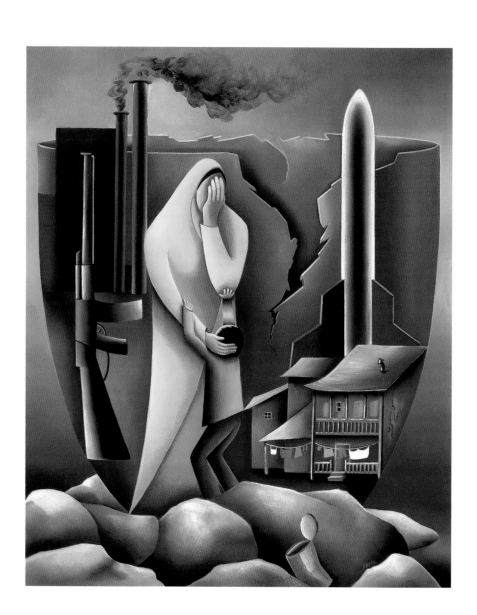

POWER AND EMPOWERMENT

A NEW STRENGTH

Evenings I kept for reading and study. It wasn't like me to be in the office after supper. But one night in the late seventies, I'd been out to a meeting and stopped at my desk on the way down the hall to check the day's mail. I was slitting the last envelope when the phone rang. I thought for a moment before answering an office phone at that hour, but when I realized who was on the other end of the line, I was very glad I had. Just that morning I had put in a bid on a corporate van to transport the handicapped. One of the major companies in town auctioned them off every year. It was this group's practice to buy vans, use them for a while, and then auction them several years later at corporate write-off prices in order to update their fleet. Everybody benefited from the process: A nonprofit organization like ours got what would have been otherwise unaffordable equipment for our own work, and the company recouped a little of the original purchase price toward new vans for itself. It was the corporate vice president himself who was calling. I was very impressed, both by the rapidity of the response and, most of all, I told him, by the fact that he himself was bothering to call about the application — and at an hour when most people would have been long home. On the contrary, he said. The bid gave him the excuse he had been waiting for to have the opportunity to talk to me.

Somewhere in the back of my mind I sensed a quid pro quo coming on. Was I aware, he went on to say without a single reference to the bid, that there was a "lunatic fringe" in our group that was making men like him very embarrassed to be a Catholic? These nuns, he went on, were holding prayer vigils in front of the downtown cathedral for all the city to see. They were protesting the increasing military budget and the govern-

ment's first-strike nuclear-weapons policy, a position he considered both indefensible and inappropriate for people like us.

"How good of you to say such nice things about us," I said.

"You completely miss my message," he came back quickly. "I am not being 'nice' to you."

"Oh, but you are," I answered. "No one has ever accused us of being Christian before. After all this time, it's such a nice thing to hear."

"You are incorrigible," I heard him say as the line went dead.

Clearly, the conversation was over. So was the bid. And that summer, for the first time in forty years, the company did not string the street banner advertising the community's annual festival.

I learned nothing about vans from that conversation, but I did learn a great deal about patriarchal power.

One of life's greatest spiritual lessons we learn simply by being born. The human maturation process is itself a spiritual event, a godly lesson. Unlike most other species, humans enter this world powerless and stay that way for a long, long time. We are born helpless. We come into life incapable of being self-sufficient. We develop slowly. Those are the lessons of a lifetime. We discover them at birth through experience and then spend all the rest of our lives coming to understand the spiritual significance of the physical reality. Whatever we manage to become at the height of our lives, between the beginning of life and the end of it, human life originates in vulnerability and ends the same way. Powerlessness is not an accident of life; it is a condition of it. There is meaning in powerlessness. There is relevance in dependency. Without it we might never grow into spiritual beings at all.

Powerlessness binds the human race above and beyond all distinctions. It transcends color; it ignores race; it reduces differences to nil. Because we will always need one another no matter how self-sufficient we think ourselves to be, the essential message of life is that we are not self-sufficient at all. We need the other.

We see the real giftedness of other people when we ourselves realize that what we need for our own well-being lies not in ourselves but in someone else. Powerlessness leads us to recognize value beyond our own small worlds. It saves us from stultifying self-centeredness.

We struggle for years to be kingdoms unto ourselves. The malady is called adolescence. It assumes unto itself everything in sight as birthright. Other people don't count until we realize that without them, we are nothing. And without us, they falter, too. Then adulthood takes over, and we take our proper place in the chain of things in the universe. Need becomes the gift that brings us to responsibility for the rest of the human race.

Powerlessness saves us from terminal egotism. We come face to face with our own frailty and, accepting ourselves, come to accept others, as well. Once we have assessed ourselves and found emptiness where we affect strength, we become less judgmental, less harsh, less demanding of others. We learn that no one is perfect, of course, but, more than that, we learn that no one deserves to be quashed because they fail to be like us. It is a powerful thing, powerlessness.

Most of all, the experience of human powerlessness teaches us that we do not need to have all power, that we will never have all power, that power is a false god. The nobility of human community lies in our enabling one another through every stage in life. Ironically, in our weakness is our strength. What we need, what the world lacks, we must hope others will supply. We must trust their goodness. We must assume their care. We must empower the power of others for the sake of all of us.

Empowerment, then, becomes a cornerstone of feminist spirituality. Without it, all the world has in each of us is one more hierarch on the way to a powerless end.

Power is one of the patriarchal world's most effective intangibles. Sometimes you see it; sometimes you don't. But one thing is sure: See it or not, you always feel it. Oftentimes, the less you see it, the more subtle it is, the more dangerous it can be. It operates in offices and titles, in webs and undergrounds, in social clubs and brotherhoods. It works through pressure and through favors. It weaves its way through the system one connection at a time. It creates a worldview in conflict with the Gospels, and it does so in the name of God.

Sociologists define power as the ability to do something whether people want it done or not. [39] People who have power don't beg; they instruct. They don't wheedle and coax; they order and they specify. They expect action and they get it. When they say that something should be done, they expect that it will be. Power works. The question is: For whom?

On the one hand, power can effect change. On the other hand, power can block change. Most of all, power used independently of the common mind and general needs of a society can render an entire population powerless. It can destroy as much as it creates, and it empowers nothing.

The spirituality of power depends on our learning to use personal prerogatives for others. It demands a reorganization of motives and a renewal of commitment to the entire human race. There is no such thing as an independent action. Everything we do leads to the next thing. Everything a powerful person does leads to something for everybody else. The lives of the powerful affect the lives of many. Their decisions make life blossom for some, unbearable for many. That's why power is never purely personal, and that's why the spirituality of power can not be ignored, our own or anybody else's either.

Power is what makes things happen. Men are raised to expect to get it — little boys get Superman suits to play in, get the right to assume their superiority, get the signal early that they can become anything they want to be. Men are raised to have power and to maintain it, either by natural right or by dint of sheer fidelity to the pursuit of it. They are raised to seek power, and power over women they take for granted. Power in the public arena they require as a mark of their own value.

The Roman patriarch, from whom the patriarchal model gets its name, had life and death control over his wife, his children, his servants, and his slaves. His word was the only word. What he declared to be the law, in a world without a federal legal system, was indeed the law. Families constituted their own legal systems, for which the patriarch, the oldest male, held responsibility till the day he died. He directed and decided and rewarded and punished. One word from him and wives were cast out, children were disinherited, slaves were executed — and that was an improvement. Not until the Code of Hammurabi in 1750 B.C. had the world even begun to conceive of a ruler who was not an arbitrary lawgiver. Society functioned on the rule of the ruler, not the rule of law. [40]

Those days are long gone, of course, but not always and not everywhere. Patriarchy is alive and well, at least in residue. It underlies the attitudes of the powerful and the systems they operate, the autocratic expectations of a democratic world, the clericalism and male prototypes of churches and families around the world. In those places, some people are in charge, and they know who they are. What's more, they know what's good for everybody else, no questions asked, no experiences factored in, no arguments heard.

From the time of the Magna Carta, the thirteenth-century charter requiring the English King John to uphold laws devised by his barons rather than to rule by his own whim and fancy, the tolerance for preemptory control began to erode in the public arena, by law if not in fact. Except where women and children were concerned. Except in the home. Except in the church. In those places, men maintained the right to absolute rule. No one, whatever the public talk of civil rights, protested the distinction between the public and the private domain. Women could not protest because they did not have the power to do so, and men did not protest because the power privileged them. The weakest of men had power somewhere. Despite the fact that they themselves felt the heavy hand of hierarchical power, they had little reason to rebel. On the contrary.

Courts all the way to the second half of the twentieth century excluded women — wives, daughters, single women, widows — from being on juries, from giving testimony in a court of law, and from entering into rights of contract and ownership. Women were not where the powerful decisions about power were being made — for them, about them, or because of them. Canon law denied women everything in the church but the right to obey. Men wrote theories of female submission and male domination and called it theology. White Western males wrote scientific treatises about race as a genetic deformity, too, and gave themselves the natural right to own people of color as well as women and children and property.

Power remained a male preserve because men had the power to preserve it unto themselves. There were also women, and we must never forget it, who profited from the patriarchal system, accepted the patriarchal mindset, and participated in the patriarchal oppression of whole races of people. They became the tokens of the system, the palace guards. And why not? The idea of inherent superiority, after all, had been spun from theology and enforced by law. The patriarchal woman ruled over women and men — most of them minorities — down the scale beneath her, lived in the luxury that ill-gotten goods provided, was, as the slave Sojourner Truth pointed out, "carried into carriages." She defended the system and trained her daughters to accept it, too. She sustained the system a patriarchy needed to maintain itself. She never became a full human being herself, of course, but she could at least live the life of a pampered child as long as being a simpering minor, a whining shrew, did not damage her own mental health. All she had to do to qualify for Barbie-doll treatment was to marry the strongest male and obey. All she had to do was to be less than she could have been as a human being.

Every day women are discovering the spiritual price of this kind of half-life, in Pakistan and China as well as in Italy and England, the United States and Canada, in churches as well as in courts of law. Every day they are discovering the spiritual absurdity of it. How can a woman possibly be fully spiritual if she is not first fully adult?

There were, of course, humane despots in the patriarchal scheme of things as well as arbitrary despots, but they were both despots, nevertheless. However they exercised the power they had — with a smile or a scowl — the fact was that both law and theology justified a man's right to control what he owned. And women and children, slaves and property, they both agreed, he definitely owned. Eventually, after centuries of struggle and revolution, the patriarch disappeared from the public throne, yes, but, despite it all, remained very apparent in the private arena.

Not surprisingly, it was Pope Innocent III who, at the request of King John, issued a document of nullification which purported to rescind the Magna Carta because it had been imposed on John against his will. [41] The barons refused the refusal — papal nullification or not — but the theory of the divine right of kings remained the philosophical basis of society, nevertheless. The power of the king, a direct gift from God, could not be impeded, the pope argued. From the theological point of view, power came, in very small doses, to popes and to kings primarily, to nobles and clerics generally, to men always, but not to every man, and never to women. Obedience to legitimate authority constituted a cornerstone of patriarchal spirituality, the final appeal, the underlying argument against everything. What authority requires, God wants, the argument maintains, all experience, evidence, or imagination to the contrary. Even now, in many parts of the world, in key institutions, in marriages here and across the globe, the concept underlies modern culture still, all theologies of humanity, all philosophies of law to the contrary.

The problem with power is not power. Obviously, the problem with power in patriarchal systems lies in the way it functions and the place it holds in the patriarchal scheme of things. Patriarchal power is exclusive, paramount, and personal, all Christian ideals to the contrary. A spirituality with those characteristics begs a reason for existence. In a social climate like that, powerful people become worlds unto themselves, cut off from their surroundings at large, impervious to the sound of the Spirit around them. They are the law. The remainder of the people have no way, no right, to do anything different — unless, of course, they too can manage to get power for themselves. To the patriarchal mindset, the purpose of power is to get more power because the only one who counts in a patriarchal society is the person at the top.

Getting to the top may be the result of charismatic charm, or it may require ruthless manipulation. It may be done smoothly, or it may be done with force. Machiavelli, in his famous work *The Prince*, which describes the ascent to and function of power in the medieval state and which is still part of contemporary textbook literature on the subject, suggests both methods. The process is irrelevant. What matters is getting there, gaining personal ascendance, becoming the center of what must ultimately be a very small universe. This kind of power cares little, down deep, for the Jesus who refused to be a military messiah, who declined to be saved by a band of angels, who gave everything he had to feed five thousand with five loaves and two fish.

Patriarchy thrives on pyramids. The problem with pyramids is that only one person can be on top of any one pyramid at any one time. In the pyramidal model, the one at the top stands alone on the backs of many. The images abound: one lion poised on the top of a cliff, one elephant leading a raging herd through the bush, King Kong towering over the skyscraper — never Jesus being baptized by John, never Jesus washing the feet of fishermen or rubbing spittle into the eyes of the blind, never Jesus breaking the bread and sharing it, never Jesus admonishing ambitious apostles.

Images come in steady stream from a history heavy with memories of power run wild. The implications of the scenes abound, too. That kind of system, stable as it may look from the outside, renders every institution internally fragile. When the power struggles start between people for whom patriarchal power means something other than the Christian model of power as service, the organization itself stands at risk of being sacrificed to rampant ambition. People with power on their minds do not have the aims of the group in mind. Not really. They simply do whatever it takes to maintain themselves where they want to be. If that requires stroking the group, they stroke. If that requires intimidating the group, they intimidate. If that requires buying the group off, they buy. They do whatever it takes to keep the power for themselves. Kings did it with chariots; modern autocrats do it with the military, the police, the party bosses, money. Husbands did it — and do it — with a heavy hand, motherhood, and economic dependence.

There is, without doubt, a lot of autocracy in democracy itself. There is a lot of autocracy in any system that takes personal power, patriarchal power, for granted. There is a great deal of talk masquerading as commitment to gender roles in this kind of society, as internal biological givens, that has more to do with power than with the sanctity of marriage and the achievement of right relationships. The fact is that biology is no excuse for oppression, for ignoring the gifts and wisdom of the other, for using people for personal comfort, personal aggrandizement, personal gain. And yet such things are done with confidence and with conviction because patriarchal power, by definition, puts power into the hands of the few. And custom and theology have kept it there.

Women, the psychiatrist Anne Wilson Schaef determined, assess every group they join to determine how to facilitate relationships there. [42] Then they begin the task of making whatever connections are necessary to solidify the group as group. Men, on the other hand, Schaef writes, analyze a group to determine who in the circle holds the power. Then they decide whether, like rams locking horns on a mountain top, they can unseat whoever has it. Or, if direct confrontation is judged fruitless, they then decide whether to join forces with the power figure in order to further their own immediate ends or to leave the group to find another. In offices they attach themselves to mentors, not necessarily out of respect, but out of the clear conviction that the career of the person above them will benefit their careers. Patriarchal power, in other words, is always personal power regardless how altruistic it may look.

Small boys are prodded constantly to get ahead, to become something, to succeed. And as they grow up, they study to get ahead, or they work extra hours to get ahead, or they join clubs they can't afford to meet the right people, the people with the power, the people who will enable them, wittingly or unwittingly, to get ahead. They do very little in life for its own sake. Girls, women, on the other hand, are never talked to about power at all. They are taught that some people are made to give orders and some people are made to take them. Women, men have decided, have a heavenly mandate to take them. Patriarchal power has no room in its mind for questions, for unconformity, or for independent women. That kind of power does not want to be embarrassed by women who confront it on street corners with moral questions that undermine the very power base that keeps patriarchy in place.

But good feminists, like good psychologists, know how pernicious patriarchal power can be. Feminist men know the seed of dissatisfaction it can sow in the male soul. The man raised in a patriarchy who does not want patriarchal power finds himself ostracized in the male community at large. Men raised in the patriarchal system who play the patriarchy game — striving, struggling, clutching at tiny offices and tinier titles to assuage their egos and earn a piece of power — find that no power is enough power to fill the gaping thirst for power. Feminist women know the oppression it breeds for the powerless. They watch women beaten to satisfy male power trips. They see the poor who work day and night to maintain the system that ignores them become increasingly poor for their efforts. They see the spirituality of powerlessness turned against them into the sin of oppression.

Feminists do not look for models of power in Roman patriarchy or clerical separatism. Feminists seek their model of power in the Jesus who threatened the system by using power for the powerless, by curing on the Sabbath, by consorting with women, and by questioning authority. To the feminist, power is an instrument to be used in behalf of others.

In feminist spirituality, power is an instrument for social good. The patriarchal mind sees power as a way to accumulate space and time and services and money for the self. The feminist mind understands power only as a way to mitigate the burdens of the other. To the feminist mind, power does not rule in splendid isolation; power stands in the midst of the proud poor to listen and to serve.

The models of power that arise out of the narrow perspective of a patriarchal worldview reek with danger. In systems in which power is more a commodity than an instrument for good, getting power and keeping it become the overriding functions of every decision. The need to keep control leads to secrecy, to manipulation, to tokenism, to ruthless disregard for others, to the carving out of unreal worlds.

Patriarchal power keeps information to itself so that others have no material out of which to fashion alternative decisions. Skewing of information, disinformation, manipulation of data, spin-doctoring become the bedrock of communication in a system that assumes itself to be the first and last word on every decision. Tokenism, the process of taking a few outcasts into the center of a system in order to keep the rest of the population out of it and to look good at the same time, serves to give an air of social change, to pacify the poor, to undermine the advocates of change. "You have to be patient," people argue. "Change takes time," they say. "Good things are happening," they contend. But nothing really changes where tokenism is practiced except that now minorities are smothered inside the system instead of outside it. Ultimately, the world inside the world that patriarchy creates blocks the rest of the world out and has no idea they're not even there. "The people have no bread," courtiers told the queen in order to explain the rioting in the streets of France. "Well, then," Marie Antoinette is reported to have said in a kind of exasperated despair, "let them eat cake!" So powerful was the monarchy of the time that it had no idea that it had no power over the people at all, that the oppressed population their power had created had long ago slipped beyond their grasp.

Patriarchal power sets out to keep people at a distance, to exclude, to control. The purpose of this kind of power is not to build the community, even when building the community is what maintains the power. Its purpose is to build a private kingdom, a power base beyond assault. Instead of stifling competition, however, patriarchal power breeds it. Pretenders to the throne crop up everywhere to jeopardize the pinpoint end of the pyramid. Where all power, all decision making, all initiative, all control come from the top, the only hope in a power-crazed society is to tear down, trivialize, minimize, or muffle anyone and everyone who threatens that kind of dominion. Power like that makes for enemies. It separates us not only from others but even from the heart within ourselves. People intent on patriarchal power don't dare let themselves get too attached to others for fear they will have to walk over their bodies tomorrow to get up the corporate ladder, to get through the social maze, to get to the top of the pyramid.

Feminist spirituality values power, too. But the feminist wants power for different reasons than the patriarchal model assumes, and practices it in very different ways. Friedrich Nietzsche, the nineteenth-century German philosopher, has been long vilified as creator of the *Übermensch* or superman concept upon which Nazi Germany is said to have built its superman theory of culture. Nietzsche was rabidly sexist, radically nihilist, and totally unaccepting of Christianity, which he labeled "a slave religion" that touted submission and set out to thwart what Nietzsche defined as man's (*sic*) basic "will to power." He did, nevertheless, make as foundation for his work, a question which, ironically, might well set the measure for any spirituality. He asked of ideas repeatedly, "What kind of people does this culture bring forth?"[43] The question is a noble one. To know whether or not a spirituality lives and breathes the mind of God, we have to ask what kind of person it would produce.

Patriarchal power, with its taste for personal ascendancy, however propitious in its spirit, creates a person bent on control, dismissive of equals, and exploitative of resources, both human and natural. The picture embarrasses for the dreariness of its scope.

There is, however, another kind of power, another way of being powerful. Feminism takes the position that for a person to become really powerful, power must be shared. Power hoarded, the feminist contends, is power lost. And power denied. A group in which the power of every individual becomes a resource rather than a threat becomes really powerful. More than simply a collection of minions, puppets, or robots programmed by the limitations of the leader, the group becomes a critical mass of individuals whose creative resources become available at their most cultivated levels. When power is shared, people become everything they can be, and the power of the group itself rises with new clarity. When power is not shared, people become objects for the satisfaction of the leader. People become dehumanized, even in the most benevolent of patriarchal environments, when their own gifts, skills, talents, ideas, needs, and concerns are simply ignored because someone else supposedly knows better. Patriarchal power cripples groups and disdains individuals. In patriarchal homes, wives too often become nameless things (the wife) or petted things (the little woman), children are invisible, and life is structured for the comfort and convenience of the patriarch. Submission masks as spirituality, and human development withers in mid-flight.

In feminist spirituality, power has something to do with self-realization but nothing whatsoever to do with the aggrandizement of the self by the suppression of others. Real feminism, contrary to variant versions that use the concept of empowerment as an excuse to reject leadership, does not abrogate power. Feminism recognizes the role of leadership and the need for power. The difference is that genuine feminism commits itself to the distribution of power. It sets out to share power and use power to make power possible for everyone else. Feminist power is a power true to the naming of twelve apostles, the sending out of seventy-two disciples, the development of house churches, and the commissioning of women ministers in the early Christian communities. It does not smack of medieval imperialism in the name of God or absolutism in the guise of the Holy Spirit.

Power in feminist spirituality maintains the right to be, the right to the self, the sacredness of the other. The kind of power that suppresses any of these dimensions sins against the creative power of God. The God who creates us to live and thrive, to grow and develop, did not create us so that we could have those rights denied or ourselves deny the same rights to others.

Misuse of power curdles spirituality at its roots. When we are our own gods, it makes God very difficult to find elsewhere in life. A commitment to patriarchal power centers us in ourselves. It treats as nothing the two great commandments upon which Christianity is based: the love of God, which honors the right order of creation, and the love of the other, which works always and only for the other's fullness of life. The right order of creation demands that each of us recognize the sacredness of the other. It is the right order of creation that tracks Cain for killing Abel, that punishes David for taking Uriah's wife, that denies the powerful a controlling power over cripples on the Sabbath. Clearly, people have a right to the power it will take for them to shape their own destiny. People deserve the resources they need to come to fullness of life, intellectual and spiritual as well as physical. Any system that blocks either of those two elements thwarts the will of God. Whatever the degree of obedience the system teaches in the name of God, a system based on the diminishment of others and the aggrandizement of self is wrong.

Patriarchal power looks into the faces of the poor and tells them to take care of themselves in a system designed to make that impossible for them to do. Blacks who are denied the right to vote, by law or by intimidation, and women who are denied the right to earn a full wage, or develop a full intellectual life, or participate in defining the theology and political philosophy that touch their citizenship and their souls are both denied the resources they need to become full human beings. Power has disempowered them. That kind of power is not spiritual. That kind of power is not co-creative.

The spirituality of empowerment, on the other hand, treats power as sacred trust and gives it away with holy abandon. It seeks always the growth of the other. It seeks always to make itself unnecessary. When executives concentrate too much on how a thing is done rather than on always teaching why a thing is being done, it is a sure sign that the capacities of people around them are being too little encouraged, too bridled for comfort. When an administrator begins to talk more in terms of *my* staff than of *our* team, there is a pyramid hiding in the psyche. When organizations set out to circumvent affirmative-action programs or hire men by choice and women for show, the patriarchal club is in full flower, regardless of the words they use to finesse the unbalanced situation.

The spirituality of power leads us to be on the side of the poor, in the midst of the oppressed, at the bottom of every ladder — sexual, ethnic, economic, and foreign — looking up. It is patriarchal power that uses vans and banners in an attempt to intimidate the powerless. It is the powerless, who value life more than they value power, who eventually take that kind of power away. When Jesus questioned Pharisees and walked with fishermen and taught women, the spirituality of empowerment was born. The patriarchy is correct: The power that empowers others is a very subversive thing.

Aggression and Nonviolence

A NEW ROAD TO PEACE

When the telephone rang, I was waiting for it. "This is Officer Somebody," the voice on the other end of the phone said, too quickly for me to hear the name. "I am calling from Washington, D.C., to tell you that your sisters have been arrested. They wanted you to know that they are all right, but it will take some time to process the group."

I could tell he was about to hang up. "Just a minute, Officer," I said. "I'd like a little more detail about this, please." It was not every day that nuns were arrested, after all. "I'd like to know precisely what happened."

"Well, Sister," the officer said, "they were arrested for disturbing the peace in the Capitol building."

I gave a little gasp. "Good heavens," I said, as if the whole situation were news to me. "What were they doing?" I could hear him shuffling a little.

"Well," he said. Well, you see.... Well, actually, they were praying the Lord's Prayer, and they didn't stop when they were told. So we had to arrest them for disturbing the peace."

I came back fast. "I'm confused," I said. "Do you mean to tell me that praying the Lord's Prayer in the rotunda of the U.S. Capitol is a felony but making nuclear bombs is not?"

"Lady," the man said, exasperated, "I don't know a thing about all of this. I was just following orders."

"Why?" I said.

"Why what?" he answered me.

"Why would you follow an order like that?"

"I have to think about that," he said.

"Indeed," I answered him, "that's what we learned at Nuremberg: We all do." Then I took the man's name and address and put him on the community Christmas-card list. It seemed the only thing to do.

We have a choice. We can go through life one of two ways. We can go booted and stomping, kicking things out of the way as we go, or we can go softly, moccasined, gently all the way. The trip will be the same. The only difference between one approach and the other will be what happens to the things we encounter along the way. We can choose to uproot the thorns and bushes in one grand show of brawn, or we can decide to nourish what is so that other things can happen as a result. The one way takes might; the other way takes strength. It is a choice that everyone makes sometime in life. Feminists, women and men, argue that the gentle way saves flowers and babies and every living thing. Most of all, they tell us, and science agrees, the gentle way saves our own lives as well as the lives and dignity of others. Socially dominant men, for instance, men who monopolize conversations, endlessly interrupt, and compete for attention — "men who attempt to gain positions of power and notoriety" — researchers at the Duke University Medical Center tell us, are 60 percent more likely than others to die of all causes. Socially dominant women, however, the same study discovers, are apparently at less health risk than socially dominant men because their dominance is achieved more by collaboration than by competition. [44]

A soul steeped in gentleness listens and learns where first there seems to be no lesson. And gentle souls are more likely to be heard, as well, since they pose little threat, agitate little of the environment, force nothing and no one into forcing back. They unmask force for the insanity it is. But we have institutionalized force, nevertheless. And to our peril.

Something isn't working. A world with more defensive weapons than the world has ever known before stands poised at all times on the brink of disaster. People with more money than the world has ever before seen live in tension. Nations with more psychologists than the world ever imagined live on a nervous edge at all times. Civility is masking as civilization. Tension is masking as peace. Force is masking as justice. Violence is masking as authority. Groups feel threatened. Individuals feel unsafe. The world is out of kilter. The spirit has gone dry. If the meek are going to inherit the earth, they had better rise up to claim it quickly.

The culture has become so divorced from spirituality that what we preach as the gospel of love at the personal level disappears into the gospel of national outrage on the public level. We wound and kill and threaten in proportions previously unknown in the history of humankind and call ourselves holy for doing so. We do all the right things in very violent ways. To discipline children, we whip them and wonder why they then become bullies themselves. We bury unarmed soldiers alive in the deserts of Iraq to save oil and wonder why the people of the globe view us with suspicion. We use chemicals to burn out visibility zones around our bases and lay whole regions waste for centuries to come. We compartmentalize personal devotion, theology, and religion — life, theory, and ritual — and wonder how it is that religion can, over time, get to be such a barbarous thing. We live a schizophrenic spiritual existence, wanting love on one level and practicing enmity at another. Feminism asks us to choose between the culture of violence and the culture of community — for the sake not only of the future but of the present as well.

An authentic spirituality does not cater to culture; it calls culture to accountability. The two concepts — spirituality and culture — are not isolates, true, but neither are they the same. Spirituality functions in dialogue at all times with the culture in which we live. It expresses that culture in its style of life and worship, it reflects its concerns, and it bears it on its shoulders, prodding, provoking, and stretching it, always intent on being more than the culture demands. But spirituality also lives in tension with the culture around it. It also, if it is genuine, challenges it. In fact, they question one another.

Spirituality tests culture for merit. Culture tests spirituality for maturity, depth, and wisdom. Without relationship to culture, spirituality has no meaning at all except, perhaps, a spurious one. To act holy is a simple thing. To be holy is the lifelong process of bringing the dull, dry demands of daily life into conjunction with ideals. That process requires patience, endurance, the strength to aspire, and the grace to grow through failure. No set of rules will do it. What is required here is an attitude of mind and a centeredness of heart.

Culture gives us one measure of humanity — too often a highly individualistic and grasping one. Christian spirituality gives us entirely another — a compassionate and communal one. The two have clearly clashed from one culture to another in various dimensions and in multiple ways, bringing new insights and exacting new responses in each. Our own period of history has come, in a special way, to the ultimate moment in the struggle between spirituality and culture. Perhaps in no other area of contemporary thought is that tension more clear than in the areas of right and righteousness. The culture is steeped in arguments in support of defensive aggression. The spiritual life, on the other hand, calls constantly for peace, for the day when "the lion shall lie down with the lamb" and "war shall be no more."

To be entangled in such cultural duplicity is to get two messages: that public belligerence is acceptable but that personal aggression is not. It is a pathetic kind of moral derangement. In a day and age when the next war has the potential to be the planet's final war, a spirituality which does not call us to examine how we work our will, both collectively and privately, fails at the core. It is at best a piety made for devotions of gossamer and lace. In a world of eleven-day wars and century-old divisions, to ignore the contradiction scorns the major questions of the day. In a society where teenage gangs terrorize adults and menace major cities, spirituality with nothing to say about violence makes a mockery of reality in behalf of a religion that is more comfort than challenge.

If spirituality is being tested anywhere in this culture, it is being tested in the arena of human relations and conflict resolution. On this topic, standard definitions of gender roles are clearly divided and with them the whole integrity of the spiritual life. The world abounds in strong women and gentle men, but, if public images count for anything at all, they are social aberrations. According to the greater body of popular literature, women are sleek and seductive or docile and submissive, and men are brawny and commanding or domineering and violent. It is not a pretty picture of either men or women. It dooms women to vacuous participation in the human race and men to a kind of malignant presence in society. Both portraits lack something. Both are caricatures of the human condition. Both are partial presentations of human beings, neither of whom is fully human, both of whom are stunted and empty. The profiles lack fiber. They belong in missing-persons files. To build a spirituality on the Iron Man and Barbie-doll images locks people into one-dimensional lives, into stereotypes that fail to reckon with reality. If humanity is genuinely good, if there is indeed glory in the clay of us, then men are not born to be brutish. Women are not born to be victims. Men are not natural rapists. Women are not sexual prey. Every culture based on the Hebrew Scripture has assumed and required the best of both men and women and then has promptly dismissed the message in favor of the expectations of the social system. On the level of the metaphysical, they argue for the glory of humanity and its links to the divine. On the level of the physical, on the other hand, social conventions make both men and women captive to categories that diminish them. Men learn to garner their gains by force. Women are left to make their way by seduction, both public and private. In the end, however, Barbie collapses under the weight of the real world. The Iron Man wilts under the pressure of adult responsibility.

Each Barbie doll-Iron Man ideal image paints half a person living half a life and, worse, unprepared for the rest of it. Images like these, however, work to the warped advantage of men and to the subordination of women. They license power and violence in men and demand inanity and submission from women. Worse than that, where force is the coin of the realm, they work to the disadvantage of the whole human race. Nations are decimated. Cultures are destroyed. People are enslaved. Whole parts of the world are impoverished by the greed of the other. In the end, women everywhere find themselves bearing children to support systems that are as much enemy to their development as they are ally, as much evil as they are good. The Spartan woman found her glory in birthing sons to fight for the city-state. Legend memorializes the ideal:

"Messenger, how goes the battle on the field?" the warrior's mother asked the courier.

"Madame, your sons have been slain," the messenger replied.

"You didn't answer my question," the Spartan mother insisted. "Tell me first how goes the battle on the field?"[45] The ghost of that Spartan mother's attitude lives still in a patriarchal world where people obey the drums of war unquestioningly and death for the state strikes a noble note.

Social psychologists and clinicians have struggled with the question of aggression for most of the twentieth century, and for obvious reasons. In this culture, the effects of aggression go far beyond minor social disruption. Today, aggression anywhere implies the possibility of escalating from regional genocide to an all-out assault on the entire planet. Ironically enough, scientists seemed to grasp the meaning of this moment for the human race before religion addressed the subject at all. It was years after Hiroshima and Nagasaki before Christianity turned its attention to the use of nuclear weapons, let alone condemned them.[46] Churches became "good citizens." Whether or not they were at the same time good Christians raises important theological concerns.

The subject of human aggression is not new, however. Freud argued that aggression was the natural death wish of the human being. Konrad Lorenz posited that aggression and violence derived from instinct, the animal side of human nature, the residue of evolutionary strategies designed to preserve the species. If those analyses were true, however, then people in general would be aggressive in general. But they're not. Quite to the contrary, whole societies have been found to be historically peaceful and nonaggressive.[47] Dollard and others theorized that aggression is a response to frustration, a cause-and-effect proposition in which frustration constitutes the trigger of a predictable aggressive response, that one leads almost invariably to the other. [48] But that concept lacks universal application as well. Many people deal with frustration and do not become aggressive at all. Aggression, it seems, is well within human control.

Geneticists hypothesized that aggression is chromosomal, but try as they might, a gene has yet to be discovered that accounts for it, and testosterone testing is equally inconclusive in both criminal and non-criminal populations. [49] In one experiment, in fact, groups receiving a placebo which they were told would raise their frustration level were actually less aggressive when provoked than the group receiving a pill which they were told would keep them calm in the face of frustration. In the first case, subjects attributed their irritation to the pill and ignored it. In the second situation, subjects assumed that if they felt frustrated in the face of provocation despite having taken the pill, then the provocation was serious enough to justify their aggression. What each group thought, in other words, had more to do with the way they responded than what was actually happening to them. [50] Theorists assume at this point that aggression may have as much to do with raising testosterone levels as testosterone levels have to do with prompting aggression. [51] We are not, it seems, captives of our chemistry.

Other social psychologists have concentrated more on what types of external stimuli provoke aggression than on its internal origins. Berkowitz argued that aggression is socially learned, that people are conditioned to be aggressive by certain social situations or symbols. In a study now considered classic, Berkowitz and LePage found that the presence of guns increased the level of aggression in a group rather than reducing it. [52] In other work, Bandura concluded that aggression was first learned by imitation. [53] What we see being done around us, in other words, we do. What children see adults doing, they do. Aggression, it appears, has social origins, not biological ones. Aggression is taught, research tells us, "especially when the prevailing sex role equates maleness and aggressiveness." [54] In cultures where men are expected not to cry and where discipline is physical, the researchers tell us, aggression is particularly high. [55] Society conditions men to violence, in other words, by limiting what a man is allowed to be in order to be thought manly by the rest of society. We provoke it. We endorse it. We encourage it. We permit it. We applaud it. And then we decry it and punish it and cluck over it.

The material makes us pause: Although some data exist to indicate that some people may be more innately aggressive than others due to chemical or physical factors, the bulk of the material and the majority of the situations require a different conclusion. Someone has to face it. Aggression is a spiritual matter to be accounted for in the things we value, the attitudes we permit, the reactions we foster, the roles we define. And those elements, in this culture, are twisted at the root, based on fabricated notions of manliness and the devaluation of the feminine, the "girlish," in life. Patriarchy devalues women; it devalues feminine responses of compassion and conciliation; it devalues the spiritual strength it takes to endure suffering and work things through and calls it weakness.

With all of its emphasis on reason, the patriarchal system seldom relies on it, it seems. What can not be effected by persuasion, the patriarchal system gives itself the permission to set out to effect by force, if necessary. Superior by definition, they — the ruling males of the human clan — reason that everything that men want and decide and define is superior, as well. It is a circular argument indeed but an effective one: Males are superior human beings because they are reasonable, and they are reasonable because they are superior human beings. And we have that on their own testimony. The intellectual merry-go-round, male fabricated for centuries, spins the whole human race into a dizzy and inescapable vortex that is called the will of God but lacks the spirit of the God who branded Cain for killing Abel, conquered cities by blowing horns rather than beheading women and children, reduced Gideon's army to one-tenth its size, and spoke through Jesus to tell Peter to put away his sword. A spirituality that blesses bombs has gone awry, has become more culture than gospel, more Peter than Jesus.

Force is the patriarchal temptation. A system organized in pyramids, on the one in control of the many, needs force to maintain it. Force works because force is so easy to apply. It is also so valiant-looking in its masquerade. Uniformed conquerors are a dime a dozen. What is lacking in the picture of the parades that celebrate them is the faces of their victims, the thousands of women made refugees, the children starved to death, the families destroyed by force masking as reason. It is called national honor, defense, manliness, reason. But from the spiritual perspective, it is none of these. It is patriarchy untempered by feminism. It is everything associated with femaleness depreciated. It is reason without feeling and feeling without reason. In systems like this, when women get emotional, they call it hysteria and sedate it. When men get emotional, they call it war and pronounce it holy.

Eventually, what is honored on the public level replicates itself in another key on the personal level. "Be reasonable, dear," so often turns to intimidation, to coercion, to violence when what she wants is different from what he wants or when what blacks want is different from what whites want, or when what the poor want is different from what the rich want. It's a do-it-my-way-or-no-van, no-banner world. Force is deaf, dumb, and blind. Listening doesn't exist in a patriarchal society. It's unconditional surrender or nothing.

Where equality lags and aggression is legitimate, life becomes a win-lose proposition in which some are natural winners and some are inherently losers. What's more, each element of the human equation inherits its status from birth, and each knows who they are. Men are meant to rule, the philosophers and theologians told us; they're the winners. Women are meant to be ruled, they argued from biology; they're the losers. Men are born to struggle for the ascendancy the patriarchal system says they must achieve, and women are born to bear the weight of those decisions. Violence becomes the stock in trade of a patriarchal system. In this model, spirituality becomes a very private thing, a panacea, a public farce.

Feminist men know the cost to the soul of such a system. They know that proving themselves too often goes the limit. Little boys fear the bully on the block who will taunt and tease and torture them until they, too, become taunters. Marines are hazed to the point of the barbaric and are expected to bear the marks of indignity with pride. Consciences collapse under the pressure either of military gangs or neighborhood gangs. Men who resist force because reason dictates that the life of feeling is a higher life find themselves forced to become what they do not want to be. The blood of our sons run in our streets because we have taught them well that violence is the answer. What, if anything, can rescue us from this kind of machoism run amuck?

From the earliest centuries, spiritual men — clerics, monks, ministers who were seen as devoting themselves to the spiritual life — were all excused from military service. [56] It was perfectly clear that a man could not give himself to the following of Christ and give over his life to the whims of an emperor who had set himself up as a god. It went without saying that a man could not give himself to the spiritual life and be in the business of killing others. "Soldiers of Christ," they called them, as opposed to soldiers of the realm. Centuries later, despite a history of crusades, vendettas, and wars — many of them called by clerics and fought in the name of God — professional religious are still exempt from national conscription. The problem such a situation creates for the spiritual life is astounding. Are there two spiritual lives, one for professional religious types and another for the rest of humankind? Is there one spiritual life that some of us live and another one that the rest of us live? Are these the same spiritual life or separate ones of different grades? The problem boggles the mind. Either a thing is spiritual or it is not.

In an environment such as this, where force is synonymous with power and power is considered a birthright, spirituality bears a great responsibility for the future of the globe as well as for the dignity of persons, for the God of the cosmos as well as for the nature of worship. The implications for spirituality are profound.

If the violence of patriarchy, defended as honor and character, is the problem, what is the Christian feminist answer to that? What does feminism offer a world at war and awash in forces that ignore the poor, manipulate the unwary, and exploit the powerless? What does feminism offer in the face of evil? The answer sets a new standard for civility. It calls culture back from the edge of its grave. Christian feminism, grounded in a theology dedicated to the presence of the divine in the human, summons the world to a new respect for the sacredness of the human body, both female and male, that leads to reverence for the total human person, regardless of sex or race or class. Committed resistance to evils inflicted on the body, whatever their forms, regardless how revered the system they represent, regardless how towering the odds, marks feminism as one of the most Christian of Christian summonses to announce the inviolable holiness of all creation. It is a long, strong call to reassess the relationship between the natural and the divine. Feminism requires a revaluation of the body and a grounding in nonviolent resistance to make that reappraisal real. Christian feminism calls the church itself to be consistent in its life ethic, to protect the born but not wanted, the born but not fed, the born but not safe, the born but not male, as well as those who may never be permitted to be born at all.

Once the body is devalued — as the whole history of Western civilization, with its pattern of large-scale genocide, enslavement, witch burnings, and holocausts attests — anything can happen. The penchant in the West to divide the ideas of heaven and earth, to demonize that which is material, to consider the body a spiritual burden rather than the place where the human soul knows the presence of God on earth reduces the body to little more than an embarrassing irritation. Our concentration is on the next world, on finding God somewhere else rather than here, on escaping the here and now and accepting suffering, even to the point of discounting it, for the sake of a better place hereafter. That kind of theology makes creation a kind of divine mistake. The impression is that God made the body but loathes it. God made the world but rues it. God made life but waits for it to be over. And most loathsome of all, the philosophers decided, was the body of a woman because it led men to sin. So much for reason, free will, and Emmanuel — God with us.

Once we deride the human body as somehow or other an obstacle course to heaven, anything we do to it stands to be ignored or at least minimized. "War is hell," we say offhandedly. "War is inevitable." "War is resistance to evil," we argue and never confront the evil that war does. "That's the way things are," we say. "Things will be better hereafter," the thinking implies. What happens here and now, therefore, is irrelevant. It's a Catch-22 kind of theology. God made us as we are but doesn't like us as we are — in which case, why value life ourselves?

Early Greek philosophers glorified the mind and spirit over the body because of the indisputable fact that the body is clearly corruptible, obviously fragile, and, ultimately, worthless, all of which conditions constituted clear proof to them that life as we know it here is inferior at base. Augustine tried to answer the question of human imperfectibility with the doctrine of original sin. Humanity, Augustine taught, is a fundamentally broken thing. At very least, he argued, things are not as good as humanity was meant to be. Since bodies sin, he reasoned, it is the soul that is superior. But it does not follow that, simply because the body provides one part of our spiritual existence and the soul another, the body is less to be honored, less to be revered, less to be seen as sacred than the soul. The division of spirit and matter does God little justice. The heaping of fault on the body, just because it is the vehicle for what the will has already decided to do, smacks of very elementary reasoning in the face of modern psychology and science. We are not at the mercy of our bodies.

Feminism, then, with its awareness of the wholeness of creation and its valuation of the female on equal terms with the male, offers us a chance to look again at the sacredness of the body. Of all bodies. The bodies of women everywhere. The bodies of Vietnamese peasants. The bodies of Iraqi children. The bodies of unborn babies. The bodies of men who are used on the battlefields of the world to maintain the systems of the world against the people of the world. When the body is valued for its filtering of the divine, aggression against it has no place.

At the same time, though aggression has no place in Christianity, resistance does. Jesus resisted evil to the end: He contended with Pilate, he warned the women of Jerusalem that things would be worse for them than it was for him if the system was allowed to remain the same, he questioned Pharisees his whole life, and he broke every law that made love impossible. What he did not do was to become what he sought to change. He did not become destructive. He did not become vindictive. He did not become mean. He became "a sheep led to slaughter," a resister who refused to bite back. And his resistance changed the world.

Feminism offers us the opportunity to resist evil without stooping to the point where we erode what we believe in by doing evil ourselves. Feminism rejects exclusion, harm, and oppression as ways to defend ourselves from the world around us. Centered in the nurturance of life and all its processes, Christian feminism offers the spirituality of nonviolence to a world that uses one generation to satisfy the inability of another one to make peace.

Nonviolent resistance, derived from Mahatma Gandhi and modeled in this country by Martin Luther King, Jr.'s civil-rights movement of the sixties, rests on six clear concepts, none of them cowardly, insipid, or weak. They are, rather, a demonstration of the kind of strength no amount of violence can extinguish. Those who identify their strength with their weapons fall at the moment the last charge is fired. Those whose strength comes from within them endure till the last cannon rusts. They are not contending with munitions, one armed force against another in the conviction that the stronger armed have greater power. They are contending with ideas, the persuasiveness of which can be contained by force, perhaps, but never destroyed by force. [57] Nonviolent resistance brings the force of conviction and self-sacrifice, a force no force can match. Nonviolent resistance becomes the only possible response for those who do not wish to become what they hate. For the feminist who lives under the pressure of domination but hopes for equality, resistance is imperative; force is impossible.

First, nonviolent resistance is pacifism, not passivism. People who are passive in the face of evil create the climate that enables it to exist. The major difference between armed resistance and nonviolent resistance is not that one opposes evil and the other allows it. The difference between armed resistance and nonviolent resistance lies simply in the means by which the resistance is waged. Both types of resistance rest on the conviction that evil must be challenged, but nonviolent resistance insists that evil must not be repeated in the effort to defeat it. Injustice done in the name of justice is still injustice. Feminism is not one force arrayed against another. It is another way of being entirely. When we sink to the level of the evil around us, we have not cured it. The strength of nonviolent resistance lies in its determination to do no harm to the other in the course of resisting harm. Gandhi wrote, "If there is blood in the streets, it must be no one's but our own."

Second, nonviolent resistance is committed to making friends out of enemies. To win a war but keep an enemy makes no progress toward peace. To win the point at the expense of the other does nothing to resolve the tension. The goal of nonviolent resistance is to concentrate on issues rather than on belittling, demeaning, destroying the people who hold positions different from our own. Nonviolent resistance calls us to distinguish between enmity and opposition. Like feminism, it demands the development of genuine feeling for the other so that we can never reduce another person, another people, to the status of "collateral damage," a term used by the military to mean the number of innocents an army destroys in its assault on military targets.

Third, nonviolent resistance condemns systems, ideas, or policies that oppress but never launches personal attacks against individuals who are the agents of those systems. Maleness is not the problem; patriarchy, that cluster of ideas and assumptions which makes men the center of the system, is the problem. If we can not assume the good will of those who oppose us, we must at least not judge their motives. Ideas and systems are bigger than any single person. To attack individuals in order to curb a sinful system only plays into the hands of the system itself by failing to focus attention where attention is necessary. We can wage war against the local mayor and miss the meaning of the fascism that makes oppression possible. We can focus on males and miss the assumptions of sexism that underlie every law, policy, and program in the world. We can turn against men and soldiers and husbands and sons and sexist women and fail to change the language, the educational programs, the economic structures, the theology that taught them to demean women in the name of God's will and moral righteousness. Hating leads to the destruction of people we learn to destroy.

Fourth, nonviolent resistance absorbs physical attack without striking back physically. Suffragettes went to jail to win the vote and never struck a blow. Women, jeered at and pummeled, supported the demands of underpaid miners by banging kitchen pans to stampede coal-carrying donkeys coming out of the offending mines. Women and men faced attack dogs in Selma, Alabama, to win the right to be human beings without themselves becoming barbaric in the process. Brave people such as these proved the power of nonviolence and the feminist commitment to respect for the other. Nothing is learned from force but force. Striking a child teaches the child to strike others. Bringing brute force to bear where brute force is possible simply teaches that might does indeed make right. Giving our bodies to the blows of those for whom physical assault is their only power to persuade does no harm to the other except what they do to themselves. Nazism exposed its most dishonorable self not at Verdun or the Battle of the Bulge but in the death camps of Auschwitz and at the ovens of Treblinka, where Jews stood silent and let Nazism speak for itself. Allied military forces may have defeated the Axis, but it was the thought of Jews standing defenseless on the edge of mass graves that quashed any possible image of a valiant Nazism forever. It was row upon row of Indians falling to their knees under the gratuitous blows of their English masters that sent a chill up the spine of a colonial world. Nonviolent resistance unmasks the inhumanity of oppression, a consciousness that is of the essence of feminism, and gives all of us another chance to repent and begin again to be thinking-feeling human beings.

Fifth, nonviolent resistance refuses to sow hate for the enemy. Hate gives foundation to hate until hate becomes a cycle that never ends. Nonviolence vows not only to end the oppression but to end the hate as well. "Love your enemy" is not poetry; it is strategy. Those we want to have love us we will have to love first. Feminism does not seek to defeat the patriarchal system; it seeks to love it to life, to dislodge it from itself so that it can join the human race.

Sixth, nonviolent resistance is based on the faith that in the end justice will come because justice is right and God is good. Two commandments undergird nonviolence and ring in every heart: The first is "Love your neighbor as yourself," and the second is "Vengeance is mine," says the Lord. "I will repay." Love is our responsibility. Justice is God's.

Each of these principles taxes courage, demands great spirituality, and promises opposition equal to the length of the struggle and the depth of the issue.

Nonviolent resistance is the weapon of those who need no weapons to be effective. It breeds questions that do not go away until governments lose the right to rule because they have lost the hearts and minds of the people.

What the world fails to understand rises to haunt it as struggle after struggle solves nothing and simply breeds the next one. In our own time, World War I, "the war to end all wars," bred World War II. The ruthless suppression of national states by Russia led in the long run to genocide in Bosnia, revolt in Chechnya, rejection in the Ukraine. The obvious has escaped us: Violence never solves anything; it simply opens wounds that fester in wait for centuries until the tables turn and the guns are bigger and the damage is beyond repair.

The idea that weapons defend a people is bogus at every level — physical, social, and psychological. To resist an enemy unarmed is no guarantee of success, true. But to go into conflict armed is no guarantee of success either. Witness the body bags in every armory of the world.

More than that, armed nations fall in brutal and pitiless ways. Weapons are no surety that a nation will not fall to external pressure. They are also no guarantee that the nation will not deteriorate from within while it stockpiles weapons but neglects roads and medical care and education and housing and employment and internal investment. The United States concentrated on defense after World War II while countries we disarmed, thanks to our insistence, concentrated on making computer chips and cars, electronic peripherals and consumer goods. Now we have new problems, not because other countries are better armed than we are but because they are internally more nonviolent or educationally superior, financially more balanced or morally more defined, while we ourselves are still attempting to recover from the militarism spawned by World War II and its effects on the soul of this nation. The question of the most militarized generation in the history of humankind after two world wars is not who won the wars but who won the peace.

Armed individuals, too, are killed despite their weapons, or, armed to the teeth, suspicious of everyone and everything, they destroy their own inner peace and openness. They make themselves targets for other people's fear. Witness the gurneys at every gang fight in the United States. Witness the eternal damage done in every family, in every relationship that relies for resolution of conflict on force. Just as the damage to human development is a high price to pay for military victory, so, too, the surrender of human serenity and personal growth are an exorbitant price to pay for enmity.

A feminist spirituality based on the Jesus who challenged the law and contended with Pilate asks no one to submit to wrong. Christian feminism asks everyone to resist evil in ways that make the world a better place instead of simply more of the same kind of place with someone new in charge.

The fundamental question of spirituality today is whether or not the spirit that rises in our hearts and overflows into our daily routine rids the world of one more beaten child, leads to a lower military budget, insists on an equality that is based more on genuine respect than on tokenism, demands a hearing for the voiceless, refuses to do harm whatever the glory of the cause, reaches out instead of striking out, and pledges to resist evil whatever the cost without doing evil ourselves.

We have come to a point in the development of humanity where the institutionalization of purely masculine values simply does not work. Patriarchy's track record is sexism, slavery, witch hunting, inquisition, colonialism, pollution, holocaust, two world wars, and now the planned planetary destruction that comes with nuclear weapons. The world is reeling from macho mania. It is a luxury we can no longer afford. Nonviolence, the strong defense of the weak, calls us beyond it. Feminism, committed to inclusion, to the sacredness of the body, to defense without violence, is not asking men not be masculine. Feminism is simply asking men not to be macho, not to buy into a patriarchal system that barters the strong and betrays the weak. Feminism is asking men to wake up and see what's missing in the picture — in themselves — and to devote themselves for the first time in history to the wholesale countenance of brain over brawn, of love over hate — the only weapons women have ever had.

It is no wonder, I am convinced, that Jesus surrounded himself with women as well as with men in a culture in which women were excluded everywhere. Jesus knew that women, the dispossessed who had nothing to lose but their spiritual integrity, were the only ones who would ever understand his gentle self, who would follow him into impossible situations and take unbearable ridicule, who would go with him despite all enemies, beyond all friends, all the way to the cross, while all the men in their company minus one huddled together in a hidden room. It is the spirituality of those strong, resistant women that is needed now.

Nonviolence won the day for early Christianity. Nonviolence is the only thing that can win it again, and, once again, women committed to the humanizing values of feminism are trying to show the way. When that happens, intimidation will cease to be a class act, and vans for the handicapped will not be held hostage to compliance with the powers of the day.

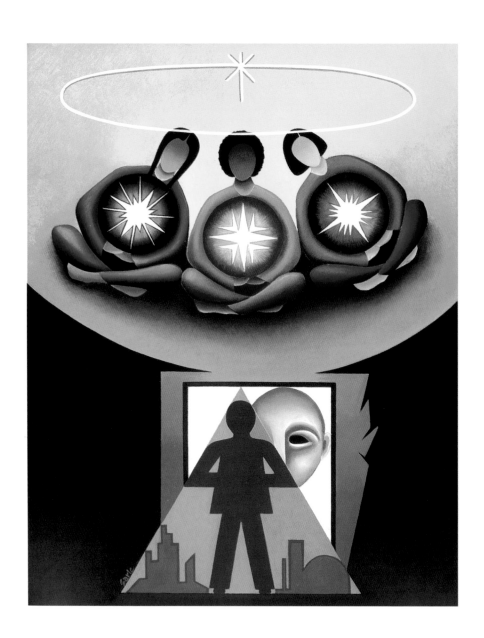

Pride and Humility

A NEW SELF-ACCEPTANCE

My mother told the story for years. It was the first Christmas after my father died. I was three, the perfect age for Christmas trees, a bad age for the death of a father. My mother's family determined to set it right. Whatever the economic climate of the times, this would be a splendid Christmas, filled with enough good things to distract us all from the real emptiness of it. I was to be showered with gifts. "What do you want from Santa Claus, Jo?" became a kind of family mantra. Obviously, anything was possible, everything was probable.

"I want a doctor's kit," I said over and over.

I remember the tree, the bright red balls, the stack of presents in the center of the floor, the family gathered to watch the baby smile. I dove for the small square package at the bottom of the pile, the unmistakable one with the sharp corners and hard top. The paper flew in every direction, clumsily, hurriedly, until there it was. I heard the laughing and the oohs and aahs all around me. I frowned a little. It wasn't a doctor's kit at all. It was a nurse's kit. "This is a mistake," I said. "This is a nurse's kit, not a doctor's kit."

"Jo," my Uncle Lou said, "little boys get doctors' kits; little girls get nurses' kits."

I remember pushing myself up from the floor and solemnly, slowly taking it over to him. "Then I don't want it," I said as I put it in his lap. "Take it back."

Some people would have called it pride. I know now that it was humility — the kind they never taught a woman in school.

If God is anywhere, the greatest writers of the spiritual life have taught for centuries, God is in us, bringing us to life, drawing us incessantly on to that place where we become everything we can be. The soul, that place where the human meets the divine, lives to develop the God-life in us here and now, to be light whatever the darkness that surrounds us, to bring us to a sense of self that satisfies without subsuming everything else in its path. The posture of the soul before a God who dwells in the heart of us to give us life, to give us peace, to give us security is at once a profound bow and at the same time a wide-open embrace of the universe. It is a mix of audacious humility and diffident pride that gives the lie to everything we've ever been told to the contrary about both.

To be immersed in God implies an accommodation with life that is less than perfect, acceptance of a world that is not organized around my ego, satisfaction with a self that is not measured by its ascendancy over others. When God becomes the core of my soul, the energy of my life, the end of my actions, the measure of my needs, every other relationship, every other perspective shifts accordingly. Then exploitation of others and aggrandizement of the self become foreign objects in the eye of the soul. The soul with a right sense of self can exist without destroying others, without consuming others in the interests of personal agendas, without destroying everything around it to satisfy itself. For the soul with a sense of God, there is something in life that is greater than the self. It is a very feminine concept, this notion that the world has a right to an existence of its own and does not exist solely for my satisfaction. It is also not a very popular philosophy in our time.

A world fresh from the discoveries of the Enlightenment and the achievements of the Age of Reason found itself with little to worship. All the absolutes, all the wonder that marked the prescientific definition of God vanished under the microscopes of the world. Elements in the laboratory and galaxies in space made the conventional concept of God difficult to maintain, if not suspect. More than that, revolt against the faith dimensions of medieval philosophy generated whole new areas of speculation in an arena once guided more by biblical premises than by human questions. In a medieval world, to be a philosopher was to be a theologian. After the Reformation and its various struggles for both political and theological control, however, religious consensus on traditional subjects had broken down. There was no unity of faith, no certainty of belief, no common commitment to just about anything that had once been taken for granted. The time was ripe. By the seventeenth century, the emphasis on reason began to change the very nature of speculation in the area of philosophy. Now, for the first time in history, humanity itself became the focus of philosophical thought, and old categories of thought began to fall away. Long obscured by concentration on notions of truth, beauty, goodness, pleasure, pain, the immortality of the soul, the nature of thought, and the preeminence of reason, the concept of the self emerged in philosophy with a vengeance.

In the early nineteenth century, the philosopher Hegel defined self as the "life-and-death struggle with the other." He argued that the self is will and power in contest with the will to power in others. Suddenly every self was a universe within a universe, the focus of action, the locus of human meaning. [58]

The implications of the emphasis on self dazzled the mind and led to whole new conceptions of life. The way was laid for the kind of personal reflection and consciousness of individual autonomy that communitarian society had never known before. The self was the center of the universe. The reasonable self, as the apex of human authority, reigned supreme. And reason, it had been well established by philosophers and theologians alike, was a supremely male prerogative.

From there, the slide to individualism and self-centeredness, to human-development theories and personal-growth institutes, to male achievement and masculine control models followed, swift and sure. Modern psychology, influenced by philosophical theories of human nature, purported to plot the profile of the self in its male and female forms with the kind of scientific precision of which philosophy and theology had never been capable. The human being was measured and surveyed and reduced to the sum total of experimental studies to the same degree and in the same manner as inert matter had become the subject of the scientific method. Men and women became definable commodities captive to responses assumed to be innate rather than societally determined. They were typed according to the roles society gave them in a patriarchal world, neither women nor men escaping without bias. As a result, two concepts emerged over time to claim the day: the biological model of male dominance and the psychological model of female deference. Men were designed by nature to be superior in body and mind. Women were designed by nature to be soft, pliable, and deficient, the servants and dependents of men, regardless of the quality of their minds. In the end, nothing had changed. A patriarchal society found what it was looking for, discovered what it had known all along. All the old assumptions were simply confirmed from another perspective: Man was the pride of the universe, woman its necessary deviation. This limiting characterization of the sexes occurred to the detriment of both men and women but most of all, perhaps, to society as a whole and to spirituality as a channel for development.

Dominance belonged to superior types, deference to their underlings. Men, the intelligent, superior beings, aspired to dominance, and woe to those men who could not achieve it. Women, the dependent, intellectually inferior part of the human race, were subsumed by the male model to serve and defer, and woe to those women who rejected the role. Pride and self-esteem became marks of mental health for men. Humility became a trait of the well-developed female. Pride became the virtue of competent men. Humility became the virtue of subordinates, of women. But, as one look at a world where the will to power threatens the human race with extinction and where the suppression of human development leads to revolution attests, the system failed. Most of the population of the world, men and women alike, are poor, undereducated, deprived of basic human services, worked like cattle, and paid like slaves. Most of the world, even in areas where the standard of living is high and conspicuous consumption is a favorite indoor sport, have become well-paid pawns in the hands of a few corporate decision makers who shape the world to their own interests. Why? What does feminist spirituality have to say to a situation in which pride runs amuck and humility becomes an instrument of oppression, in which life has never been better and, at the same time, never been worse on such a massive scale?

When things clearly aren't right but nothing seems to be obviously wrong, what is the problem? When achievement is the disaster of our lives and domination its obsession, what is the cure for the demon that possesses our souls? When our relationships break down time after time after time, what is the emotional barrier that accounts for it? When we lack a sense of enoughness and spend our lives striving for what we do not have, where can we possibly find peace, feel serenity, take hope?

Ironically enough, the cure may not be in the twentieth century at all. The cure for both personal dis-ease and national chauvinism may lie in looking again at a spirituality of right relationships based on a far more ancient model. Thousands of people across time have thought so. But if there is any truth whatsoever to its spiritual durability, then the world may need it now more than at any other moment in history.

There is clearly something missing in North American priorities. There is something wanting throughout the Western world, in fact. There is, as a result, something missing in many lives. Everybody seems to know it; nobody seems to know exactly what it is. Some people say it's good old-fashioned family values that have been lost, like togetherness and frugality. Some people say it's moral discipline that we're lacking and set about demanding tougher judges and longer prison sentences. A few people lament the demise of patriotism and religion and a respect for values in general, but, for the most part, the qualities they grieve — nationalism and blind obedience and parochialism — are more fanciful than real in a world of high-tech equipment, rampant individualism, globalism, and space travel. The fact is that some things are simply lost forever, like the Pony Express and drugstore soda counters and parish novenas. Early in this century railroads and refrigeration and education took their toll on what had once been a largely local and one-dimensional world. Now the world is changing even more.

The problem is that just because the world is different now does not mean that it is better. With the changes have come public confusion, psychological disorientation, and personal turmoil. What is really valuable in life? Where is peace?

The truth of the matter is that, though we may be suffering from what we have lost in this generation, we are also suffering from what has increased in it as well. In a culture of computers and cars and personal independence, we have not only bartered stability in the society; we have also added to it a touch of despair, a tinge of frenzy. The planet is in orbit; the country is in orbit; families are in orbit. People move from place to place and fad to fad and idea to idea. Everything is in flux. Everybody is going somewhere for something else. Everybody is scrambling. Everybody is straining and stretching to get more of something: more things, more security, more status, more power.

It is a high-tension, high-achievement, high-anxiety society. The question is: What caused it and what, if anything, can cure it? The answer, perhaps, is not that we have gotten too developed, too sophisticated, too educated, too wealthy; the answer may simply be that we have gotten too much into ourselves, given too much of our lives to the self, gone too far off center in our lives. It isn't what we have that is so much a problem. It is what we do with it and what it does to us. In this case, perhaps, the things we have acquired have become blinders on our souls, jangle in our minds, confusion in our hearts. What we have really lost is the sense of who we are and where we belong in the universe and what that means for everything we do.

Benedict of Nursia, the founder of Western monasticism, taught in the sixth century that pride is the basic flaw in the human system and that humility is its corrective. [59] Benedict made the keystone of his rule of life a chapter on humility that he wrote for Roman men in a patriarchal culture that valued machismo, power, and independence at least as much as our age does. Pride, ancient spirituality says, is the corrosive of the human soul. [60] Humility, the Rule of Benedict says, is an antidote to violence and a key to mental health.

But humility is not a contemporary North American virtue, and pride is a very male thing.

Popular psychology, in a vital attempt to correct the distortions of low self-esteem that derive from a warped sense of sin, a misunderstanding of perfection, or the vengeance of an angry God, has concentrated on building a sense of personal worth in the human psyche. If humility has something to do with being passive, meek, and self-effacing, those are not qualities that a generation schooled in human development calls healthy, let alone smart. But the correction comes with its own set of problems. As a consequence of total concentration on self, it has become individualism and getting ahead that we are too often most concerned about, not the cultivation of the globe, not the needs of the entire human community. Concentration on the self alone and the compulsion to achieve can bring in their wake, ironically, a troubled sensitivity and a constant sense of failure.

But modern psychology alone did not undermine the cultivation of humility in contemporary society. It is also true that for too long in religious literature we substituted an allegiance to humiliations for a commitment to humility, as if one were the other. *Humility* and *humiliations* are not synonyms. Humility, spiritual manuals implied, depended on humiliating exercises designed to break the human will in the name of holiness rather than on the liberation that comes with freedom from the self. Humility, Arnauld, the founder of Jansenism argued, requires arbitrary deprivation of the human spirit, as if humiliations were not the very seedbed of the anger, resentment, and spiritual agitation that rise to plague a soul that has been denigrated rather than developed. [61] The results of that kind of military discipline are both spiritually and psychologically disastrous. What is more, they have serious social consequences as well.

Thanks to the machinations of a male-based psychology, pride and humility are sex-biased qualities. One is for men; the other is for women. Clearly, pride and patriarchy are a volatile mix. One feeds on the other; one makes the other imperative. For men, pride is the keystone of the patriarchal system. A lifelong commitment to patriarchal power depends on pride for its fuel and confirms it in its achievements. For women, a false humility, concocted to maintain a narcissistic system, is the counterfeit coin parlayed in place of the real thing. Patriarchal pride exaggerates the worthiness of men; patriarchal humility perverts the worth of women. Men live pride.

Women live a humility that distorts their full spiritual development and justifies their social limitations.

But humility — real humility — is a good thing, a vibrant thing, a wholesome thing, a freeing thing. The fact is that everyone has something that controls his or her entire life. For some, it's ambition; for some, it's greed; for some, it's dependence; for some, it's fear; for some, it's self-centeredness; for some it's narcissism — that exaggerated sense of self that diminishes everything around us. The patriarchal system takes pride in control, in superiority, in power, in consumption of the resources around it. The patriarchal system envisions a world where some of us, men, assert personal, exclusive, and total control of personal space through some kind of conquering and conquest, no matter how benevolent. To the patriarchal system, independence, accumulation, and status are moral ends to almost any means.

The feminist man who does not espouse the patriarchal vision, who prefers a simple life in community for the sake of internal development rather than a professional career bent on wealth, image, and public recognition, finds himself on the edges of life. Systems disdain him; other men avoid him. Responses such as his from a man, they call abnormal, lazy, weak.

The woman who finds herself immersed in such a system discovers two things. First, she finds out that patriarchal pride is insatiable and must be fed at all times. It's called "stroking the male ego." Second, she discovers that there is no place for her in the patriarchal picture. If women perform as well as men, the behavior is considered decidedly unfeminine. If men concentrate on professional development in addition to family ties, they are considered ambitious. If women give themselves to career advancement as well as family relationships, they are considered abnormal. Women have learned to downplay their achievements rather than to celebrate them, to apologize for their energy, their intensity, their interests. Men take it for granted that male interests, needs, and concerns will take precedence in every situation. What's more, they take it for granted that the primary responsibility of every woman in life is to see that men's needs are met. The patriarchal system has taught both women and men very well. He is a full human being, and the world belongs to him; she is a unique human being and exists to maintain it.

The spiritual effects of such a system are stultifying for both. Men find themselves enslaved to unreal expectations about themselves, their role in life, and their rightful place in the universe. Caring for others requires a discipline of major proportions when the consistent message has been that other people exist to take care of you. Giftedness in others becomes a threat to personal well-being. Exaggeration becomes a terminal disease and narcissism an ever-present danger. There is little room for anything in life — including God — but the self.

Women, on the other hand, learn in such a system that, though they are usually tolerated in life and often loved, they are seldom respected for themselves, for their opinions, for their talents, for their perspectives. The life of a woman shrivels under the weight of an unnatural deference and lost development. Women live knowing that inside themselves is a capped well, a fount of untapped treasure, a person gone to waste. The spiritual life of a woman never knows total maturation in an environment that never seeks her opinions, her interpretations, her insights, and her experience of God. Whatever ministry she was born to perform never comes to light, is lost to the church, dies on the vines that were never cultivated.

But what can be put in the place of a pride that consumes everyone and everything around it, and what does that have to do with a feminist view of the world?

The twentieth century has plenty to relearn about humility, and the Rule of Benedict, with its stress on feminist concepts in the face of a culture committed to male dominance, may be its best model. This ancient spirituality identifies twelve degrees of humility, twelve levels of personal growth, that lead to inner peace, to the achievement of a state of mind that renders us capable of living a truly human life with other human beings. What is just as important, perhaps, is the fact that the twelve degrees of humility lead to other things as well. They lead to self-development, and they lead to community consciousness. They lead to equality and mutual respect. They permeate all of life, quietly and unobtrusively and totally. They call men to human community and women to personal development. They call all of us to come to know ourselves for what we really are no matter who tells us differently. They justify doctor kits for little girls and new ideas for men long accustomed to only their own.

In 1980, for the first time in the history of the association, the American Psychological Association named narcissism in its catalogue of psychological disorders. The narcissist, the diagnostic manual says, amplifies personal achievements far beyond their objective value and exaggerates personal problems, as well. [62] Whatever claims they make about themselves, in other words, narcissists make to the ultimate. So absorbed are narcissists in their own agenda that they find it almost impossible to sustain emotional relationships with other people. They themselves are the begin-

96

ning and end of what is important to them; they can't possibly be sensitive to, aware of, or concerned about someone else. On the contrary, they have a consuming sense of entitlement. If there are awards to be given, positions to be filled, promotions to be achieved, they expect to receive them and are uncommonly wounded when they do not. Every story circles back to themselves. Every comment refers to them. Every situation features them before the conversation is over. The needs and abilities of others they view with scorn, if they view them at all. Little if anything is important to them beyond themselves. They are social cripples with little or no capacity to accept personal responsibility for personal shortcomings. Most disturbing of all, perhaps, the manual describes the syndrome as often impervious to treatment. Given the client's penchant for unreal self-evaluation, that may, unfortunately, be all too true.

Narcissism consumes a person with self. The American Psychological Association calls it a neurosis, a personality disorder that leads to social disfunction. At the same time, it is also surely a by-product of a system that demands competition, ambition, self-aggrandizement, and superiority as a matter of course. Narcissism is the patriarchal disease. Preening becomes an accessory of the system. Scorn is its natural counterpart. Self-centeredness measures the rest of the world and finds it wanting. What else but the will to patriarchy could possibly fuel such wholesale ambition, such derogation of the rest of the world? The heart sinks at the thought of such institutionalized disorder. What can possibly correct it?

The Rule of Benedict, one of the oldest documents in the Western world to deal with humility, confronts a patriarchal society with humility as the major counter-cultural witness of the age. It endures in the history of spirituality to this day as an antidote to a disorder of the human heart. The context in which the rule was written may be its strongest lesson. Benedict was writing a rule of life for men, not for women, in a world given to male hierarchy and independence. By developing this new form of religious life around obedience, community, and humility, Benedict called Roman men, who had been formed in a totally patriarchal society, a society that institutionalized power, hierarchy, and dominance, to a clearly feminist spirituality. Humility, this ancient spirituality insisted, requires the ability to learn from others, to be part of the group, and to understand and accept personal limitations.

Humility in the Rule of Benedict is not subservience. It is openness to the totality of life, both within the soul and within the human community. From a Benedictine perspective, humility does not diminish a person; it provides a basis for realistic evaluation, for accepting who and what I am, for being willing to grow beyond my demanding self, and so for allowing other people to be who and what they are. This kind of humility requires a new kind of self-acceptance.

Humility, according to the rule of Benedict, rests on twelve principles or degrees of development that cover the gamut of human existence and confront us relentlessly with the notion that human limitation is the gift that relates us to God, to the world, to the self, and to others. [63] Pride drives a wedge between us and reality; humility is its glue.

Humility, the principles imply, has something to do with our relationship to God, our openness to people, our expectations in life, and our attitudes toward others. The program is deceptively simple. In actuality, it would turn both spirituality and life upside down.

Humility, the Rule of Benedict teaches, requires first and foremost what the ancients called the *memoria dei*, "the awareness of God," at all times, in all places, at the center of all things. It is so easy in a patriarchal society to make ourselves gods of the tiny little kingdoms we occupy. We climb very small ladders and then assume that we have risen to the heights of our humanity. The realization that God is god and that we are not requires serious reflection. Striving for all the tops of all the pyramids in the world will not change the fact that no person ever really reaches the top of anything and that the real acme of creation lies deep within the soul and waits for us to bow before it in awareness and in praise. Those whose lives are lived without listening to their hearts, those who make themselves, their work, their status, their money their god, never find the God of the universe, who waits quietly within for us to exhaust our compulsive race to nowhere. Unlike everything else in a patriarchal world, God, according to the Rule of Benedict, is not a goal to be reached; God is a presence to be recognized. Men need the first degree of humility to curb the delusions of grandeur inherent for them in the system; women need it to realize that the presence of God is as strong in them as it is in any man. Real humility, based on the will of God for creation, leads women to reject oppression, not to accept it. The willingness to be defined by others for their own convenience, the indifference to the invisibility that comes from exclusion from the boardrooms, the synods, the decision-making centers, even from the pronouns of the language, and the lack of a sense of responsibility for women who are in these situations with no one to help them, no one to speak for them, no one to care become postures inconsistent with the first degree of humility.

Becoming aware of the presence of God within us, then, ranks clearly as the first characteristic of humility. The second degree of humility, that we "love not our own will," that we trust that God's will for me is what is best for me, is its corollary. These are impelling words. They raise the question of how it can be argued that the God who made women and men as two sexes of the same creature wills development for men and diminishment for women. Humility reads the will of God in creation and learns from it. God has a will for the welfare of all creation. We have no right to wrench it. When we can accept the obvious will of God for us, we learn to accept life and live it to the hilt. God's will for the universe, rather than my will for the universe, becomes a constructive way of thinking. The need of one group of people to subvert another group of people for its pleasure, its profit, its comfort, its convenience becomes clear for the obscenity it is. The need to consider myself the standard, the gauge of life, diminishes. The rationale for patriarchy disappears.

At this second level of humility, we stop being in charge of the world. We learn to live life to the fullest and applaud it in others as well. In this degree of humility, men are called to recognize that they are not the norm of humanity. Women are called to live up to the potential that is in them. The second degree of humility teaches a patriarchal world that none of us, male or female, is either the last word or the only word. Each of us provides only one word of the human dialogue with life. For the rest of it, we must learn to listen — men to women, women to men, and all of us to the word of God that's in us. There is so much glory to be missed in the world if we miss the will of God in it either for ourselves or for others.

Benedict's stages of humility call us to live in accordance with what is God's will, not simply to submit passively to someone else's will for us. At the same time, in the third degree of humility, to "submit to authority," Benedict tells the seeker in the spiritual life that omnipotence is a quality that must be consciously forsworn. By recognizing that there are people in my life who have a claim on my behavior — wives on husbands, authority figures on personnel, parents on children, officials on citizens — we find a therapy for arrogance. There is no such thing as absolute authority, mine or anybody else's. There are only multiple authorities in different dimensions of life, to whom we owe a privileged hearing. To refuse to recognize someone else's right to help us construct our worlds is to live a very lonely life cut off from the wisdom and care that those around us are required to provide for us.

Beyond the insights of legitimate authority, however, there is a wisdom that comes from opening our minds and hearts to the world at large. Accepting the authority of those who have no official authority over us — the middle-aged son who listens to his father, the professional expert who accepts the recommendations of the team, the experienced manager who accepts the expertise of the younger executive, the husband whose wife is his head as well as he is hers, the man who seeks direction and takes counsel and listens to advice and admits to error and weakness and uncertainty, the woman who learns to respect one man at a time rather than patriarchy for its own sake — joins us to the human race. And deserves its support. To listen patiently, and endlessly, to others — learning from them — without cutting them off, without cutting them down, without mocking their ideas, gives us the right to be listened to ourselves. God's will is alive around us in the minds and thoughts of other people. Only by learning to listen to other people do we save ourselves from ourselves. A man's sin against the third degree of humility is to assume that his independence gives him the right to be a woman's authority just because she is a woman. A woman's sin against the third degree of humility lies in accepting authority without seeking at the same time to shape it, to stretch its vision, to test its truth, and to hold it accountable for its consequences.

The fourth degree of humility, to "endure direction and not grow weary" even when the situation is difficult, requires growth in internal discipline. Running away from the hard moments in life solves nothing, the Rule implies. We need guides. To be our own light is to have dim direction. Men in a patriarchal society find themselves required to prove their value by proving their independence. But arrogant autonomy makes for devastating effects — on marriages, on businesses, on the society itself. Life is too important an enterprise to be in the hands of any single person. There is simply too much to know for any one person to know it all. We need help, and seeking it is not a sign of weakness.

Relationships crumble under the strain of power struggles. In order to merit the right to hold power, it is imperative to give up struggling to assert it before we have the kind of internal strength it takes to qualify to use it. Violence will stop only when we learn to learn from others and to control ourselves in difficulty. Men are called by the fourth degree of humility not to use force as a substitute for patience. Women, the missing members of every institution, are called to be patient in the struggle for personhood but to refuse to bear the unbearable, as well. Patience with an ongoing process is one thing. Acceptance of abuse is another. To bear abuse, injustice, and invisibility is not virtue; it is the sin of passive compliance with evil.

There is, at the same time, the need to develop the ability to work things through. Always to compete for immediate preeminence, never to accept guidance, constantly to demand instant results, instant gratification, is the mark of a spiritual adolescent. Real spirituality lays up strength for the long haul. Patience and perseverance hone us for those moments in life when there will be nothing we can do but wait, when there is nowhere to go but here, when there is no way to impose my will on the world. Laying down personal power enables me to benefit from the power of others, to accept direction so that I can learn to function without it, to gain self-confidence, self-control, and insight.

Men who are denied the right to defer to others become social bullies. Women who are expected always to defer to others rather than to learn to exercise power themselves become trapped in small worlds, half developed, only partially alive. A world where men rule unilaterally and women bear the results is a world out of kilter. And we do. And it is.

The fifth degree of humility, Benedict says, is to let someone know us, to confide in someone "any sinful thought entering our hearts or any wrongs committed in secret." Striving always to appear to be something we are not leads the soul into a morass of emptiness and dissatisfaction. The masks weigh heavy on our hearts. What we seem to be we are not; what we are we do not want to be. We live our lives behind darkened windows. We pretend. We embellish circumstances and stretch details. We hide and parley and play with facts. We lose sight of ourselves. If there is no one with whom we are completely truthful in life, we are not truthful at all.

Self-revelation is the beginning of growth. Self-knowledge corrects. Once we open our hearts to another, the charade ends. We are saved from the burden of having to be perfect anymore. We get the opportunity to compassionate with others. "Who is it that we wouldn't love if only we knew their story?" [64] Mary Lou Kownacki reminds us in her collection of monastic mantras, *The Sacred and the Simple*. Once we admit to another what we have always known inside ourselves, then we can come to peace with ourselves and with the rest of the world as well. Not before.

It is humility, not pride, that makes us fearless. Once we ourselves have admitted who we are in the secret places of our hearts, who is it that can diminish us? Self-righteousness dies, and simplicity and equality rise to take its place. For men, the call of the fifth degree of humility is to honesty with themselves and with others. Bragging can stop; self-sufficiency can stop;

entitlement can stop. Men can learn to accept the human condition — and admit it. They can simply put the universe down and relax. For women, the fifth degree of humility is also a call to honesty. They can admit their gifts and come to see them as a piece of God's will for them; they can stop waiting to be called on and begin to volunteer the answers they feel inside of them. They can take responsibility for the resentment, the anger, the anger they feel at being overlooked, underrated, and outtalked. They can turn the sin of false humility into honest participation.

The sixth degree of humility, the Rule of Benedict teaches, is "to be content with the lowest and most menial of treatment." Hoarding things in order to create a public image smothers life before it ever starts. When enough is never enough, happiness is always just out of reach, and unrest is pervasive. We set out to buy status by buying things. "I have; therefore, I am" seeps into the psyche and shapes the soul into nothing but a plastic profile of myself. It is an empty existence. Humility, the grace not to put on airs, restrains us from substituting things for character.

The truth is that, whatever the patriarchal delusion, there is no such thing as entitlement — for anyone for any reason. We must learn to grasp life lightly, to look for its essentials rather than its baubles, to loose ourselves of things that clutter the soul and tie down the spirit. If we can possibly learn to be contented with less, we can never be frustrated again, never insulted again, never ashamed of our cars or furniture or clothing again. Freedom calls. Humility disentangles us from the burden of the unnecessary. Men are called by the sixth degree of humility not to spend their lives on anything less than what a life is worth. Women are called to take their minds off the externals that have become the measure of a woman and to insist on the resources it takes to develop the person within themselves. Men are called to accept the mundane circumstances that make life go round — the shopping, the washing, the care of small children — and take personal responsibility for them. Women are called by this degree of humility to insist on spending less time on the window dressing of life and more time on becoming everything God calls them to be in a culture that calls them to less.

Humility frees us to make no exaggerated demands on the universe, to live with more soul and less greed. A patriarchal world touched by humility could learn to live with less oil, less money, and fewer toys. Wars for gadgets could be over forever.

The seventh step of humility, according to the Rule of Benedict, tests Western patriarchy to the marrow. It is the step most often misread in the name of psychological theory, most totally rejected in the name of modern social science. It is the degree that cuts to the bone. The seventh degree of humility, the ancient text asserts, is that we not only say but really believe that "we are inferior to all and of less value...." The patriarchal mindset rises in revolt. The woman's mind recoils from the message she has sought all her life to throw off. And rightly so. Yet, unless we face our basest selves, unless we see that we, too, are created from the same clay as the rest of the world, we run the risk of thinking just the opposite. The seventh degree of humility tests the other six. After we have recognized the presence of God, surrendered to God's will in life, accepted direction from others around us, unmasked ourselves to ourselves, endured the discipline of patience and the urgency of justice, and developed a sense of proportion, comes the moment of truth: We, too, all of us, are human, fully human, not members of a one-person superrace, not immune to anything. No, the real truth is that we, too, are capable of the worst in the human condition. Self-acceptance is not the right to say to the world, "Too bad. That's the way I am." Self-acceptance is the obligation to say to the world, "Forgive me, friend. There is so much more that I can be." Both women and men are called by the seventh degree of humility to realize within themselves the grace of glory that comes with the grace of recognizing one's own need. Men need to recognize their needs. Women need to bring their needs for personhood, presence, and power to light so that the world has access to all of its resources, unblocked by groundless invisibility and sinful deference.

The seventh degree of humility ties us to the human enterprise, links us to the rest of the human race, requires us to think in terms of circles rather than pyramids.

The eighth degree of humility is that we do only those things "endorsed by the community." We are invited, in other words, to learn from experience, to value wisdom figures, to follow in the wake of those who have tried life and found it navigable. We can stop reinventing the wheel. We can cease to act as if the world depends on us. We can stop calling attention to ourselves and simply join the stream of humanity at its best. We are immensely weak, the seventh degree of humility reminds us, none of us, male or female, beyond the pale of the human condition, and so, the eighth degree of humility instructs us, we need models; we need support; we need teachers. The patina of patriarchal independence disappears. We are called to see the glory of God in the other and to learn from it. Gone is the great-man theory of history. History is not one man anywhere. History is history. It is the story of all of us, none of us to be forgotten.

Given from this perspective, humility becomes the foundation of foundations, the spackle of communities who see themselves as a people, remember the best in themselves, and set out to maintain it. People who use a group for their own purposes destroy it. People who forget the wisdom of the group in favor of their own whims sacrifice the group to a private god. Self-worship is the beginning of cruelty to others. If I am superior, I can do what I will to others. Women in a patriarchal society have known the truth of that for centuries. Only a consciousness of brokenness opens us to what is good in others. It is my unrehabilitated self that is tender, that is kind. When I see my own limitations, when I see the goodness in others, when humility comes, violence ends.

According to the time-tested wisdom of the spirituality of humility, consciousness of God, openness to direction, self-knowledge, and a sense of otherness shape the soul of a humble person. But attitudes are not enough to make for a world of equals. Behaviors matter. Behaviors signal what we think about ourselves — and what we think about others. Benedict singles out four of them in particular.

The ninth degree of humility, this wise psychologist argued, is that we "control our tongues." The blustering has to stop. The commands have to stop. The criticizing has to stop. None of us is anybody's god. None of us is anybody's patriarch. Others do not exist at our fiat, and we can not extinguish them, verbally or otherwise. What we need is reflection. Talk without thought is useless. What we may need most is interior quiet in a culture of boom boxes, agitation, and perpetual motion. We need space to think in a culture bombarded by sound, most of it vacuous, much of it extraneous, a great deal of it self-centered. We have a culture forever geared to mending the way we talk when it may be silence that is lacking.

Silence is not an empty thing. Silence is full of what we need to learn about ourselves. The angels with which we each must wrestle reside in the silence within. If we are to come to fullness, it will be silence that teaches us what it is about ourselves that must be healed. The adversaries within us with whom we have yet to contend, the strengths within us which we have yet to release are all exposed by silence. Without silence, we risk the possibility that everything else we do will be nothing but sound and fury. Humility lies in discovering what we really think, what we really fear, what we're really worried about, what we really want to do in life. The questions are within us; so are the answers.

Silence also makes us accessible to others. When I am able to resist announcing myself, I can listen to others. I can hear what they're trying to say to me. I can listen to them for their own sakes. The first step in relating to others depends on my knowing myself so that I can listen to others with an honest heart. The relationship of silence to humility and of humility to equality is plain for all to see: The first step in becoming a humble member of the human race, in tempering the arrogance that patriarchy breeds, lies in silence. To be true to the ninth degree of humility in a patriarchal world, men must learn to listen; women must learn to speak the silence that has been imposed on them for centuries, without apology, without timidity, without fail.

The tenth and eleventh steps of humility, then, follow naturally. The tenth step of humility is that we "are not given to ready laughter," the eleventh, that we "speak gently and without laughter, seriously and with becoming modesty." When we know ourselves, cruel laughter aimed at others ends. The quality of our laughter is a measure of our sanctity. It tells us how we feel about others. It tells them, too. More than that, laughter tells us what we think about ourselves, whom we think we're free to judge, who we think we are. Why we laugh, the way we laugh, and the things at which we laugh say more about ourselves than they do about whatever it may be that provokes it. A sneer and a smile are not the same thing. A document that was clearly written for men in a barbarian age rises above the cultural level of that age and brooks no misunderstanding of the relationship of laughter to humility. The bawdry and the brutal are not humor. There is no boys-will-be-boys philosophy here, no tolerance of locker-room language, no assumption that girlie jokes are innocent humor, are acceptable commentary. The tenth and eleventh degrees of humility order us to take life, all its facets, all its peoples, seriously. The tenth and eleventh degrees of humility bring patriarchy with all its derisiveness, all its ridicule, to its knees.

Humor and laughter are not necessarily the same thing. Humor enables us to see life from a fresh perspective. It gives strength, insight, and sight. Benedict does not forbid humor. Benedict forbids the garrulous, the thoughtless. Benedict insists that we take our humor as thoughtfully as we take our life so that the lives of others are not impeached by it.

Finally, the twelfth degree of humility describes the human being with the humble heart. The twelfth degree of humility, the Rule says, is that we "manifest humility in our bearing no less than in our hearts." Bearing comes from the soul. Presence itself is a message. Communication theorists tell us, in fact, that over 80 percent of every message is communicated nonverbally. What I believe in my heart will show in my body. It's in the strutting, the agitation, the seething, the disdain that corrupting, damaging, demoralizing pride shows. It's the "Daddy says" look on a husband's face; it's "the Terminator wants" look on the bully's face; it's the "because I said so" look on the face of the boss who intends to intimidate, who expects to be obeyed, who humiliates and depreciates and exploits the other that signal pride where humility should be. It's also the wilting, the withdrawal, the agitated hovering in a woman that belie a false, a damaged, and deficient sense of humility.

Pride is patriarchy played out in a democratic world to remind its underlings who's really in charge. Humility brings us, instead, to the presence of God, the wisdom of others, the authenticity of the self, and the esteem of the other that make life, the world, a good and gracious space. It is the preventative of bitter divorces, abuse in the home, disparagement in the workplace, ethnic wars, domineering relationships, social derision, classism, sexism, and global exploitation.

Benedict of Nursia was a man with a feminist soul in the midst of the most macho of cultures. He brings us all, women and men alike, to realize that in the softer side of human nature, in the cultivation of the mystical, nurturing, poetic side of life, lies the key to equality, to respect, to spiritual maturity, and, perhaps, even to the preservation of the planet.

Universalism and Otherness

A NEW FOCUS ON THE SUBJECT

The church sits in the middle of the block on a main street in a suburb of Dublin. The locals call it the parish church, but it has all the style of an American cathedral: massive interior, circular dome, life-size statues, Persian rugs, and a marble baldachin over the deep-set altar. I found myself looking around the church during lulls in the services, caught by this, fascinated by that. On one wall was a series of memorial plaques, not the ornate kind so often found in English churches to note the baronial benefactors of an area, but impressive nevertheless. They were carved in marble, every major letter gilded. They were meant to be noticed. Two of them behind the altar rail caught my eye at Communion after Communion. "What's wrong with this picture, what's wrong with this picture?" I could feel myself wondering as I followed the slow line up the aisle to the Eucharistic minister. Finally, one Sunday morning, I stayed after Mass to study them more closely. And then I knew what it was that was meant to be noticed, what it was that had been troubling me.

The first plaque read, "The Altar of Christ the King is Erected by Canon Fleming, pp, *in memory of his mother, who died 8th of* September 1935. *Pray for them."*

The second plaque read, "Pray for the soul of James Clarke, *died* 22nd of May 1933, rip, *in whose memory these Stations are erected by his sister* Mrs. T. Farrell."

Both plaques were ostensibly raised as memorials. The one in honor of the woman carries the name only of the man who donated it. The woman in whose honor the gift had been given was honored with a plaque but not with an identity. The second plaque, donated by a woman, names the man being honored first, unlike its counterpart, and then, at the end rather than the beginning of the memorial, names the woman donor herself.

There it was, carved in stone, embossed in gold: the total invisibility of women — even when women were noticed, even when a woman was supposedly being honored.

A world without a soft heart lacks any reason to exist. In that kind of world, the important things — natural beauty, human bondedness, honor, honesty, suffering, kindness — will get lost in the shuffle somewhere along the line. That world goes blind with business, loses sight of the human dimensions of the daily, forgets that life rides a cycle of gain and loss until all the bric-a-brac of time which we collect as we go along drops away and only the important things are left. We learn too slowly in such a world. But, in the end, some things are plain: bank accounts have nothing to do with a person's last hours, let alone the quality of their lives. Power melts between our fingers like sand in an hourglass, worth nothing when we need it most. Reason gives way to feeling with terrible intensity. At the end, only the self remains, whatever that is, whatever composes it, whatever makes a person what they have become — hard or soft, loving or rigid, intolerant or receptive, righteous or forgiving. A spirituality that lacks heart lacks quality of life. It is the terminal disease of a patriarchal society. It barters the soul for the system.

Somehow or other, in the course of human development the world has shifted away from a sense of indomitable hope in a nurturing and never-ending creation. Instead, contemporary culture has fallen captive to realism, even to pessimism, to the myth that life is tough, a dog-eat-dog exercise that inevitably gets harder as life goes on. The conclusion may be correct. Perhaps it does. The problem is that few people ask why. Why is the Garden of Paradise wilting? Why is it that people who work all their lives find themselves poor in old age? Why is it that marriages break down in great numbers? Why is it that the ozone layer is ruptured, that climate is changing and coastlines are unsafe? The answer may well be that all these things derive from choices and values long harbored by this society and long destructive of it.

The values driving Western society, social scientists tell us, are profit, personal comfort, exploitation, control, individualism, and dominance — all of them a blueprint for disaster. [65] When profit rules a people, means and ends too often get confused, and human beings are sacrificed to make the margin wider. When personal comfort ranks first in the human agenda, the life circumstances of other people whose lives depend on ours dim and cloud and drop from view. Charity dies, and compassion goes sour. When exploitation takes hold of a people, every relationship becomes a deal, every deal becomes a scam, every scam becomes deadly. When control seeps into an environment, personal agendas take precedence over group agendas, individuals are reduced to things, and the things become cogs in someone else's wheel. When individualism becomes pathological and community becomes nothing but a stepping stone to private ambition, the human condition wastes away into one long series of internecine struggles, good for no one, damaging to all eventually. When dominance replaces equality, a society loses the gifts embedded within it. It finds itself limited to the abilities of only one segment of the group rather than energized by the creative energies of all of it. Where does a culture get ideas so small, so smothering? What can possibly be missing in a society that would lead it to take such a self-destructive route in the first place?

The answer, I think, lies in the principles of exclusion that underlie patriarchy no matter how benign the patriarchy seems to be. The ostracism of women as a class from public policy and the longtime elimination of women from the theological development of the Western world have limited the vision of the world. Patriarchy makes discrimination generic. It entombs half the people of the world. It makes profit, personal comfort, exploitation, control, individualism, and dominance normative. The problem lies in the invisibility of women in a patriarchal world.

The riddle of human existence haunts the history of philosophy. The earliest of pagan philosophers wrestled with the topic. Whole philosophical schools formed around the question of how human beings came into existence. For some, creation implied an outpouring of creative energy, an emanation of the creative force, an expression of the god-force itself. [66] For others, the explanation was that we were created out of nothing since the divine force could not be lessened and still be divine. In Scripture, however, the answer is a far clearer one. However we are made, Scripture teaches, we are made "in the image and likeness of God." We are, all of us, in other words, sparks of the divine. We are all fragments of the face of God. We are each a particle of eternity. We are, together and alone, expressions of the divine in time.

The ideas overwhelm. If Scripture means what Scripture says, then humanity is nature alive with the energy of God. Human nature is more than nature; it is divine presence and eternal possibility in embryo. The concept charges our ideas of life and human community with new meaning. If we are all made in the image of God, if we all spring from the expression of the divine, then every human being born brings an intuition of God to us. The ideas fix the heart in a kind of perpetual awe. In fact, those ideas rooted the mystics in wonder. Francis saw God in the leper. Catherine of Siena saw God in the poor. Benedict saw God in the guest. The poet Gerard Manley Hopkins in his poem "God's Grandeur" wrote, "The world is charged with the grandeur of God/ It shines out like shining from shook foil...." Thomas Merton had a vision of the presence of God in the passersby on a busy street corner in Louisville, Kentucky.

We are, if we are to take Scripture seriously, surrounded by the presence of God in one another. The implications of that kind of theological worldview turn the social system upside down. If we are all words of God, then we all have something to say. We are all a message to the rest of the world of the nature and mind of God. We are all expressions of divine presence, of divine hope, of divine truth. We are all meant to be word to one another.

The feminist challenge to contemporary theology is a simple one: Whose word will a woman be? Her own or someone else's?

The great irony of the spiritual tradition lies in the fact that, though it has customarily divided the knowledge of God into two parts — intellectual and affective, head and heart — and identified women with the understanding of the heart, it has at the same time denied those insights. Spirituality was the province of men. Men decreed its substance, taught its principles, and promulgated its standards. The theological insights of the great spiritual women of the world stayed locked away in the depths of their hearts, the subject of no synods, the concern of no schools. Women's experiences of God were defined as matters of private devotion. Women were bodies, not essentially spiritual beings as men were supposed to be. In fact, the relationship of women to the spiritual life was seldom seen at all except perhaps at the local level of influence, where they performed the ministry of community or maintained the devotions of the age. Historians tell us that over the last ten centuries, since the High Middle Ages, relatively few women have been named saint and the greater proportion of those who were date from periods in which the recognition of sanctity rested on popular acclamation rather than on a canonical process. Between 1000 and 1900, according to Philip Sheldrake, about 87 percent of saints were men, 13 percent women. What's more, he notes, the improvement in the number of women since that time has been marginal at best. In this century, 25 percent of those canonized have been women, 75 percent men. [67]

It is precisely woman's experience of God that this world lacks. A world that does not nurture its weakest, does not know God the birthing mother. A world that does not preserve the planet, does not know God the creator. A world that does not honor the spirit of compassion, does not know God the spirit. God the lawgiver, God the judge, God the omnipotent being have consumed Western spirituality and, in the end, shriveled its heart.

As a result, religion is a nowhere land for women, even in denominations which ordain women, and the world is all the poorer for it. The imaging of God, the definition of God, the meaning of the Scriptures, and the nature of spirituality all belong to men. There are the exceptions who prove the rule, of course: the Julians and Catherines and Hildas and Radegunds and Hrotswithas and others who emerged to make their mark on the spiritual life of the world simply because they were figures too strong to be ignored. No doubt that thread of spiritual history exists not only to be reclaimed but also to be developed. Nevertheless, all in all, whatever the effects of women on popular devotion and public ministry, it was the male authorities who ran the schools, the male writers who produced the textbooks, the male priests who interpreted the faith, the male church that wrote the rules that purported to determine the nature of the human race without benefit of the insights of half of it. It is a sterile existence for a woman. It is an even worse state for the world as a whole.

The omission of women from the defining developments of the faith leaves humanity at large, churches in general, authority collectively with only half an understanding of who God is and how God functions on which to draw for understanding and inspiration. It blinds all of the world to the insights of half of the world and gives us the image of half a God.

The problem, of course, is that what does not live in consciousness can not thrive in the society around us. The values and images that derive from the male definition of God are harsh and severe ones. They reflect the patriarchal system out of which they emerge. God the king, God the warrior, God the patriarch, God the Lord weigh the world down. They bind women to subservience. They release men to rule.

If the creation story of Christianity demonstrates anything at all, however, it demonstrates that men and women have been distinct creations from the very beginning. They were irrevocably related to one another — bone of bone, flesh of flesh, yes — but at the same time conspicuously separate. They were discrete. They were explicitly different, discernibly the same. In the mind of God, obviously, one did not exist to subsume the other. On the contrary. And yet one did.

To be saved, the church taught for centuries in both its patristic writings and in the works of the Reformers Luther and Calvin, women had either to become manly, asexual, or obedient to a man in marriage and given to childbearing in order to redeem themselves from being female. [68] It is difficult to underestimate the effect of the theology of original sin on the role and status of women in Western society. The male became the representative of humanity; women became its spiritual scapegoats, deficient by nature, warped in will, unequal in intelligence, a necessary mistake.

In 1598, a treatise by Valens Acidalius entitled "A New Disputation Against Women in Which It Is Proved That They Were Not Human Beings" set off a new round of debate on the subject that lasted almost one hundred years. [69] Theologians, doctors, and lawyers argued the subject during the same period and with the same intensity that Europe was at the same time also debating the full humanity of American Indians. The last academic trial on the question of women's humanity was held in Wittenberg in 1688, when Lutheran theologians refuted it. But the text and the responses to it continued to be published into the late eighteenth century. It was clearly a burning issue.

Physicians eventually pronounced the female sex normal in itself — in contradiction of Aristotle's argument that women were "misbegotten males" — but pronounced them physically inferior, nevertheless. Lawyers denied them legal rights on the basis of mental inferiority. Theologians denied them spiritual rights on the grounds that they were daughters of Eve, the one responsible for the Fall, as if Adam, too, had not fallen in the face, apparently, of the weakest of enemies — which leads any thinking person to wonder about Adam's ability to manage anything.

The downward spiral of women in patriarchal culture, a culture given to the preeminence of father figures over the mother-god of earlier civilizations, dizzies the mind. The world surrendered its heart in deference to an addiction to power and lost feminist spirituality with it. Spirituality, our conscious personal attention to the God-life within and around us, has, as a result become more a matter of public ritual and personal rule keeping, moral and ecclesial, than of personal development, lifestyle, and spiritual growth in concert with the world around it. It is hard to know now where the circle began — in theology, which then influenced social theory, or in social theory, which then shaped theology. Whatever the chain of events, if there is one, one system parallels another; one sphere has legitimated the other.

Contemporary psychoanalytic theory, developed by Freud and elaborated on and amended by Jacques Lacan in the twentieth century, defined women either as the sex in lack or the sex against whom the male child needed to struggle for separation in order to be whole himself. Whatever the explanation, the conclusion was the same. Women were incomplete beings whose very existence threatened men. "Woman: The Eternal Primitive,"

William J. Fielding called her in 1927.[70] That kind of thinking, buttressed by male-biased theological interpretations, set the terms for the role of women in the spiritual life and for the defeminization of the spiritual life at the center of the church. Women simply disappeared from the public arena, the theological platform, the social center of the world. Men became the ultimate exemplar of humanity, women, a lesser version. The results are plain to see. That whole attitude of mind has come home to roost in a world listing toward an irrational rationalism and a church on the dangerous edge of having deprived itself of the feminine vision of God.

This drive to universalism, to the imposition of the male mind on all of humankind, to what feminist philosophers call the creation of the universal subject, deprives the world at large and men in particular of a feminine perspective on life and faith.[71] Men, long trained by a system that defines them as hard, as reasonable, as tough, as intelligent, as natural leaders, play the role whatever the cost. Men have no opportunity — no right — to be frightened, to be weak, to be feeling human beings. If they want to succeed in a patriarchal world, men must become worlds unto themselves. As a result, for a man, being wrong becomes more preferable than being weak — translate: being soft. To be wrong is simply to have been misled; to be weak is to be womanly. The spirituality of the feminine, the notion that there is a part of God that is not intent on the discipline of the soul but on its nurturance, finds little scope in male theology and less in male spirituality. For men, asceticism takes the place of trust, repentance takes the place of growth, sin takes the place of wholeness, control takes the place of vision, and authoritarianism takes the place of search. This kind of male spirituality, long taught and long touted, is an arid and depressing road to the God of life.

What is worse is the fact that a corollary of patriarchal culture is that men become whatever they are at everyone else's expense. Universalism leaves men bereft of the fullness of humanity, yes, but it makes women invisible. In a patriarchal society, men speak for women; men make laws for women; men make decisions for women; men subsume women into themselves. Women become the being who is a nonbeing, a display piece, an ornament of life, but never the essence of life. Early feminists said that women had been made into sex objects, and that is certainly true, but the situation is far more fundamentally serious than that. The truth is that woman, in a man's institution — and most institutions are men's institutions — the most honorable woman of them all, is no object at all. She simply does not exist.

The basic assumption of a patriarchal society — that men know what's good for women — sounds the death knell for any concepts that men themselves do not recognize, do not find engaging, or do not support. Women's ideas seldom if ever come to light as independent issues. Studies show repeatedly that topics raised by women at a conference table, in those societies where a woman's presence is even tolerated in such gatherings, go unrecognized until restated by a man. [72] Then, presented by a man, they become topics. Then they get heard. Then they get addressed. Ideas die daily as a result, not because they lack merit, but simply because they are women's ideas and the merit of them remains too often unconsidered. A woman, the Western world, the Western church, told itself philosophically, taught theologically, and structured socially, is simply not worth the intellectual and spiritual attention of the male world.

The spirituality that emerges out of a culture like that is not only deficient, not only hinged on false assumptions; it is of necessity warped. What happens to the spiritual life of a young girl who is made to understand, consciously or subconsciously, that she has no place in the spiritual domain except as a consumer of someone else's God? What happens to the spiritual life of a young man who learns clearly that he is the vessel of election on whom the world depends when he knows what he does not know but can not bring himself, does not dare to admit it? What happens to creativity and truth, to feelings and humility in those cases? What happens to the spiritual life of a world steeped in sermons and short on vision?

Finally, the uniqueness of women as women gets lost entirely in a culture which has been taught to assume, as a matter of course, that men embody the fullness of humanity, the totality of humanity, and the entire vision of humanity. To men, the other dimension of the human race is not a woman; it is another man.

The symbolic evidence of woman's invisibility in the human race is most clear perhaps in her suppression, her camouflage, her negation even in language. Women are subsumed, excised, erased by male pronouns, by male terminology, by male prayers about brotherhood and brethren, even and always by exclusively male images of God. The tradition that will call God spirit, rock, key, door, wind, and bird will never ever call God mother. So much for the creative womb of God; so much for "I am who am." So much for "Let us make human beings in our own image, male and female let us make them." What kind of spirituality is that? To take the position that using two pronouns for the human race is not important in a culture that has thirty words for *car*, multiple words for flowers, and dozens of names for dog breeds is to say that women are not important. Is that what spirituality is all about?

To function as if women were not an equally endowed, absolutely imperative intellectual part of the human enterprise and its spiritual process sins against otherness, subjectivity, being as being, and God as the creator of two fully human and equally intelligent sexes. It reduces the human race, made by God to be distinctly two, to only one. It shrinks the glory of creation to the paucity of maleness. It deprives us all of the fullness of human intelligence, the breadth of human perspective. It deprives us of a full view of the human landscape, full awareness of the spiritual backdrop of life. It leaves us with a stunted spirituality at best. No spirituality can be whole when the vision that inspires it is only partial.

The loss to the human race and the spiritual tradition of the enrichment, depth, perspective, and fullness that the full equality of women would bring to every institution leaves the world listing heavily toward destruction over development and the churches more concerned with law than with life. Women's experiences differ, by and large, from the experiences of men. Women know life differently than men do and enrich it accordingly. To lose women's experiences to the grist of human decision making is to lose whole levels of understanding of God's way with us. Women provide a different plane from which to view the human enterprise. They bear it in a different way and bring to it a different agenda. They bring another depth to the human endeavor. Women read the Gospels from a different perspective than white Western male clerics do because women's place in the social order to which Jesus is speaking differs radically from that of privileged males. They read from the perspective of the woman with the issue of blood, of women in the crowds on the mount of Beatitudes, of women at the foot of the cross. Women are the missing dimension of the church. Without them spirituality becomes a shell of the possible. The soul sinks at the thought of the imposition of such limitations in the name of God. The Jesus who was born of a woman without the intervention of a man shakes his head in disbelief at such a perversion of creation.

Feminist spirituality would bring to the church a new sense of presence, of vision, of understanding. Feminist spirituality brings with it a new image of God to liberate both women and men from the God of the medieval courts and ancient battlefields, the rules and the stopwatch, the transcendently distant and the powerful masculine.

The feminist image of God derives from the face of God who lives in the icon, Jesus, the Jesus who bowed his head before John and felt sorry for people standing in the noonday sun, the Jesus who refused to be saved by angels and brought life to those dealing with death both in body and in heart. This dimension of God is humble and feeling, nonviolent and empowering. Jesus, the feminist image of God, cures and loves, is vulnerable and receptive, laughs and dances at wedding feasts, cries tears and feels pain. This glimpse of God is the glimpse of otherness at its ultimate. It is in this model of otherness that the feminist puts hope for equality, for recognition, for respect, for the end of sexism that is the end of a healthy spirituality.

Otherness, the realization that the insights and experiences of women are valid and valuable, that women are adults to be reckoned with, thinkers to be sought out, creators to be encouraged, full participants in the drama of life, autonomous moral agents in the progress toward a fully moral humanity, measures the quality of any spirituality. Otherness determines the caliber of male-female relationships and is the real arbiter of the authenticity of any spirituality we claim to have developed in the history of Christianity.

The world needs respect for otherness, not simply patronizing approval. The world needs the voice of otherness in order to hear the cries of the whole human race. The world needs the presence of otherness to redeem it from its headlong plunge for profit, power, comfort, control, individualism, and dominance that sears its soul and gives the lie to a spirituality of the fractional.

Woman is the totally other other. As long as a woman is allowed to be less than she should be, a man will be expected to be more than he can be. Until the patriarchal system realizes the insufficiency of the principles of power upon which it is based, the disconnectedness of its bias for maleness from the real composition of the world, and its need for a spirituality that embraces otherness rather than excluding it, it can never become whole. It will continue to fall under the weight of having to carry a burden for which it is only half prepared. The real tragedy, of course, is that we will all suffer for the loss of a sense of otherness. More, underneath it all, spirituality itself will lead at best to half the image of God.

Authoritarianism and Dialogue

A NEW LEVEL OF CONSENSUS

I remember the discussion very well. More than that, I remember the shudder of caution that went through me at the thought of what was about to happen. Whom should I warn: him or them? The man or the women? In the end I decided that the women didn't need a warning. These were the seasoned types. There was no worry. They would not allow themselves to be taken over. The man, my friend, was the one who was going to have the hard time. A priest for years, an ex-World War II serviceman, a complete gentleman, and a professional with the avuncular qualities common to a bachelor relative, he was facing what could well be the hardest assignment of his life.

He had been named to a national committee of religious treasurers. Their task was to set up financial guidelines for religious communities throughout the country. In the style of men everywhere, he already knew, he told me, what the guidelines had to be. Meetings weren't necessary. His guidelines could just be sent to the committee and voted on, but the women — "You know how women are. They want to 'process' everything" — insisted on meeting to discuss them. A waste of time. A total waste of time, he figured. "I don't know if I'll be able to stay with this thing or not," he said. "I don't mind hearing what people have to say about something, but sooner or later somebody has to have the right to make the decision." That's when I shuddered. SomeONE was not the way women made decisions these days.

The year slipped by. I had managed to avoid conversation about the committee for months. Better to let the little things go, I thought, and save a friend or two along the way. And then, one day, out of the blue, without my asking, he said, "You know, I learned a lot on that treasurers committee. It really worked, that process stuff. I didn't like it when we

121

*started, but by the time it was over, everybody there was satisfied with the
results. And did them." I could hear the wonder in his voice. "I've never
had that experience before," he said and narrowed his eyes. "With guys
you always have to either force the ones who don't go along to comply or
just plain ignore them. But these women worked the guidelines all out
together. And did them. It took more time to get them written," he
mused, "but in the end they really did them."*

*He was standing there, arms folded across his big chest, staring over
my head into space. Thoughtfully. Very thoughtfully. I knew he hadn't
figured out the difference yet. What do you do at a time like this, I wondered, laugh or cry?*

In the last fifty years the face of the world has changed. From one perspective, the globe has gotten bigger. The United Nations, which was built to
hold fifty-one nations, now includes over two hundred separate political enti-
ties. At the same time, by another level of measurement, the globe has grown
smaller. People who never for a moment thought that they would ever leave
the city in which they were born, let alone the state, let alone the country,
now travel freely from one spot on the planet to another. They go on business; they go for vacation; they go for study; they go simply to see what the
rest of the world is like. In the same way, the population of the globe has
broadened, and the population has also narrowed. In 1776, at the time of the
American Revolution, two-thirds of the world lived under the domination of
white Western powers. We were a few people consuming the rest of the people. In 1945 more than half of the world still lived under colonial governments. Today less than 1 percent of the world is not self-governing. Whites,
once the isolated center of the human race, are less than 5 percent of the population of the globe. The direction of the human race, in other words, is no
longer being determined by the old questions common to the West, by old
agendas essential to the West, by old centers of power, either in Rome or now
in Washington. The world is a new place in which to live. People are being
brought together at every level, from every corner, through every medium.
Communication is drawing the entire world into a single vortex. The Inter-
net alone has all the earmarks of being the most consequential development
in human communication since the invention of the printing press. The total
democratization of communication is possible — and now at hand.

The implications for social organization of changes such as these shat-
ter centuries of givens. The world is not white: The classification of people
into higher and lower species based on colors, beginning at the top with

white, simply does not wash in the face of the complexion of the entire human race. The world is not male: Half the population of the globe is female, visible or not, and far more than that if anyone bothers to consider the females who are not allowed to be born or are abandoned at birth to die simply because they are female. The world is not Western: The West, in fact, is Johnny-come-lately to the roll call of civilizations, many of which were rich in culture and learning before the West had so much as discovered fire. The world is not Christian: Only 16 percent of the world is any kind of Christian at all. [73] The ideals and ideas, the values and the vision defined by Christian civilizations are not the ethical, moral, or social cornerstones of the rest of the world. There are other ways to look at things besides from the perspective of a Christian cleric. There are other ways to evaluate things besides the capitalist system.

The implications of those premises for the development of human community are even greater than their effects on institutions and political systems. Given this kind of demographic profile, the concept of community takes on dimensions previously unheard of in the history of the human race. Suddenly community does not consist of making consort with someone just like us. That, in fact, constitutes a ghetto, not the gathering of the entire civil society. Community, on the other hand, implies the ability to become one with someone who is not just like us. It takes adjusting to, this notion that we are not superior, not first, not primary, not right, not the first word and the last word at the same time. Life is a circle, not a square or a triangle, we have learned at the negotiation tables of the world. We do not sit atop the system and guide it to right answers — ours. We have now only the right to join the group and work on common issues together.

The implications of massive social change for the principles of spirituality go even deeper than they do for institutional development and community identity. The expansion of the rest of humanity into what has traditionally been a white world means that we must learn to live next-door to people who go to mosques rather than churches, to temples rather than chapels. We simply do not have the luxury now of the four-hundred-year time span it took for Catholics to adjust to Protestants. There is no Peace of Augsburg now to divide us geographically as once it separated Catholic from Protestant territories in Germany. There are no crusades left to preserve the territory of the Middle East from the heathens. There is no battle of Lepanto that will drive color once and forever from our sight as it once closed Catholic Europe to Islam. Like the Tower of Babel, the world has been mixed now, once and forever. Issues will not be decided anymore simply from the point of view of a Christian heaven, or eternal salvation, or divine incarnation, or the Ten Commandments, or the sacraments. Instead, all these things will now be put to the test in us as never before. Now spirituality will wear a real face.

Goodness, virtue, and respect for life now take on new meaning for us. We will come face to face with Buddhist concern for enlightenment, with Islam's call to unity, with the Hindu sense of the sacredness of the universe. We will come together as seekers who meet at a convergence of life paths to continue the pursuit of life together. We will meet the other in new and exciting ways — unless, of course, a patriarchal past makes a feminist future impossible.

What is needed in a world where differences become the norm is a spirituality of dialogue, of openness, of coming to hear in the other the voice of God spoken in a new key. Feminism depends on being able to listen to the one in whom we would not expect, in a patriarchal system, to find truth, wisdom, insight, direction. It throws open the barriers endemic to patriarchy and stands no gatekeepers guard over the deposit of questions therein. Feminism invites questions, questions assumptions, assumes nothing. In feminism all the little people of the world gather with the great as equals. In this system, control matures into leadership, and leadership thrives on facilitation rather than suppression. Openness becomes the watchword of every feminist discussion, and no idea is factored out before it is explored. To the feminist mindset, the pursuit of truth becomes more important than the pursuit of law. Feminism abjures hierarchy in search of possibility where it is least assumed to be. Openness derives from respect for the Holy Spirit, a concept long taught in Christianity but little lived in its patriarchal form. There is only limited room for the Holy Spirit in a system that depends for its existence on control, thought suppression, and the nullification of questions.

Patriarchy by its very nature requires control. However benign the despots, they are despots, nevertheless. In a system such as this, authoritarianism is both the mainstay of patriarchy and its cardinal virtue. In patriarchy the system counts above all else. Order rules, not wisdom, not charism, not vision. Persons come to power by virtue of the system, not simply by virtue of public support. Persons exist to maintain the institution so that the institution can maintain the person. The pattern never ends. In a patriarchal world persons do not support persons; they support institutions. What is good for the system is assumed to be good for the person, but what is good for the person is not assumed to be good for the institution. In patriarchal marriage the norms of the institution are structured to maintain the family structure that serves patriarchy, not to assure the development of all the members of the family in such a way that the institution of marriage as we know it would itself change. It is on the backs of women that the patriarchal family and the economic system rest. Those institutions exist for their own sake, and woe to the women who would change them in ways that would make life as fully achievable for women as it is for men.

In such a society, loyalty and obedience become archvirtues. Men, note well, made wedding vows promising to "love, honor, and cherish" a wife. Women, on the other hand, were required in the same ceremony to promise to "love, honor, and obey" a husband. The very compact of the system left no room to doubt the hierarchy of persons in it, however much talk there was about the partnership of marriage. A patriarchal system rides on obedience, blind obedience and absolute authority. Nowadays, the word may be "Trust me," but the message is "Obey."

The problem of obedience in a patriarchal system touches more than questions of individual development, however. The problem lies in questions of conscience. When the laws of the system, any system, take over, the Law above the law stands at risk. Conscience pales in the face of common belief. The sounds of the system smother the sounds of the prophetic. In a patriarchal world, where some are invested with natural power and others are denied it, the law of the fathers conflates with the Law of God. Then it becomes impossible to tell one from the other. Then, eventually, there is no difference at all between one and the other. Then conscience is reduced to memory of the rules rather than pursuit of the ideal — whatever the law itself says to the contrary, whatever the people think, whatever the system aspires to at its best, whatever the gospel demands to the contrary.

The moral pyramid in an authoritarian world rests on reward and punishment determined by the supreme patriarch and levied by the system. It is the kind of system that crucifies without cause, except perhaps the one accusation that exposes the process: And Pilate said, "I find no cause in this just man." And they said to him, "This one makes himself equal to the Law." This one, apparently, has too much conscience for any system to control.

Authoritarianism, defined as an excessive drive for concentrated authority, is not, interestingly enough, a personality trait; it is a personality syndrome. [74] In other words, people are not born authoritarians; they become them. Authoritarians are formed by authoritarian systems, and the patriarchal system, a breeding place for control, forms them best. The profile of the classic authoritarian conforms to conformity. First, for whatever reason — approval, security, love — authoritarians themselves submit with great docility to established authority figures in their own lives. They ask no questions, rock no boats. They are the good children of every system, the patriots of the state, and darling daughters of the church, who earn their way through life by never questioning it. Second, they punish aggressively those groups whose condemnation is endorsed by established authority so that authority as they know it does not fall. As children, it becomes a matter of throwing stones or hurling epithets at the minority neighbors their parents do not like. As adults, it involves promoting legislation to punish the outcasts of the society in which they live. They want no civil rights for homosexuals, no hospices for AIDS patients, no subsidized housing for the poor, no parole program for prisoners whatever their ilk. They want the system at its traditionalist best, the perfect for the perfect. Finally, they become the conventionalists of the society, intent on maintaining the social system established by the authority figures before them. They internalize the system. They become the system. They commit themselves to the preservation of the system whatever the current forces to the contrary. They are traditionalists with no cause besides tradition.

Authoritarianism, long noted by social psychologists for its effect on the social system in which it exists, shapes personalities as well as institutions. [75] Authoritarians, the researchers say, do not tolerate ambiguity well. The unknown is not comfortable space to them. They want answers. Men, research confirms, invariably outscore women on authoritarianism scales. Trained to conform in sports, clubs, and student corps designed on military models, they come to expect the same. [76] The notion of letting things work themselves out, of working things through, of seeing how things go, is a foreign land that offers no future to an authoritarian. Maintaining what is, what was, what has been tried and valued in the past becomes the norm. It is also psychologically comforting to many. Extreme conservatism, psychologists say, is a strong ego defense against insecurity and a fear of personal inferiority. The formula is a simple one: If I hold on to what I have been told by authorities before me is correct, I too will be correct. The thinking isn't always wrong. On the other hand, it isn't always right either. Without the flexibility to review things with an open mind, to decide between the two, the world may never know which is which.

The consequences follow. Authoritarians want things under control. Most of all, they don't want things to change. When things are "right," they want them kept that way. Not surprisingly, then, authoritarians score higher than most on rigidity, inflexibility, and dogmatism scales. They see things in simple terms. They know what is right, and they demand it. As far as the authoritarian is concerned, a thing is black or white, right or wrong. There are no in-betweens, no mitigating circumstances, no reasons to change. They punish for wrongdoing. They argue that people get what they work for. They believe that people get what they deserve, and so they blame poverty on poor people, alcoholism on alcoholics, AIDS on homosexuals. [77] The social intimations of such a mindset ring an ominous bell. Authoritarians know the rules, keep them, and condemn those who don't.

Raised in a rigid, intellectually stifled environment where questions are forbidden, experimentation is suppressed, and deviation is punished, children become rigid. It is a lose-lose game. The system loses, the person loses, and the society loses from the lack of creative thinking, the loss of openness to the Spirit. But there are other effects of an authoritarian environment that touch the very core of Christian spirituality.

Religious belief and authoritarianism, studies show, go hand in hand. [78] The religious believer who is untrained in the theology of the faith and formed only in its customs and cultural expressions looks for the current rules rather than the reasons for them and clings to rules uncritically. One thing this person knows for sure: It is the rules that save. To change the conventions of the faith in midstream amounts, in this mind, to the destruction of the faith. For some, the end of the midnight fast before Communion, the lifting of the ban on eating meat on Fridays, the change of language in the *Book of Common Prayer*, the presence of women on the altar spelled the end of church affiliation for them. For the authoritarian, it is following the map, not making the journey, that counts.

The link between personal development, the forces of the culture, and the characteristics of the spiritual life that emerges from the relationship among them becomes increasingly clear. To the authoritarian mentality, the world divides neatly into two groups — in-groups and out-groups — and the out-groups are plain to see. Out-groups are the people who are not like me and who are, therefore, manifestly inferior. [79] They live the wrong way; they believe the wrong ideas; they do the wrong things. Spiritual corollaries follow logically from that kind of thinking. Control, reward, punishment, judgment, and submission dominate the environment. Prejudice takes the place of principle. What has always been must be, even in the spiritual life, sometimes most of all in the spiritual life. Then anything done to the group called "out" is acceptable. Harassment, ostracism, torture, war, and death all become instruments of glory and, often, instruments of religion.

The need to control ranks paramount to those whose aim is to preserve a system of thought, a codex of belief, a charter of behaviors. They brook no negotiation with the norms. They use rule books as their Bibles. The recipe for the Eucharistic bread, the rubrics for the liturgy, the language of the Mass carry more weight with some than the theology of the Eucharist itself. To the authoritarian, what is done is far more important than why it is done.

Reward and punishment come swiftly in authoritarian environments. The God of authoritarians is a God of judgment, swift to punish and slow to forgive. The most common symbol in ecclesiastical art during the period of the Black Plague and the Hundred Years War became the image of Christ the King, scepter in hand and rule book at the ready. Surely such suffering was the result of sin, the image implied. [80] God the judge had struck a mighty blow in the interests of salvation. Obviously, the way out of the quagmire of adversity in which the world found itself mired was to repent, to submit, to become docile again. Authoritarianism masks easily as spirituality: the virtue of a righteous people in the service of an avenging God. It showed itself in the past in Crusades, in witch burnings, in slave brandings, in wife beatings, and in jihads. Today authoritarianism is on the rise in the West again, most virulently demonstrated by ethnic discrimination, physical and legal violence against homosexuals, and vehement antifeminism. [81] Indeed, in this time of great social change, authoritarian moralism is alive and well, producing a cold and apathetic people who are contemptuous of weakness, suspicious of compassion.

The spirituality spawned by authoritarianism is a barren and sterile excuse for the God who leads us gently on from one discovery to another in life until we come to fullness of soul and soundness of heart. It is patriarchy pretending to be holy. It resides in unholy righteousness and rests on legalism. It freezes theological development. It misses the mystery of God and puts limitations on the Holy Spirit. It denies that creation goes on creating in life and that revelation, growth, and insight come with time, develop with time, and depend on time to bring them to fullness.

There is, however, another path to God that goes through life open and aware, full of awe and committed to finding God wherever God is and especially where I am sure God can not be.

Feminist spirituality puts another face on God by putting another face on people, as well. To the feminist, every human being comes to us as an expression of the mind of God, worthy of respect, valuable in themselves, capable, competent, and effective. The one who is other, who is different from us, comes to us as angel, as messenger in the guise of a person. Each has, in the feminist mind, the potential to be the visitor to Abraham's tent, the guest in Benedict's monasteries, the envoy to Mary the mother of Jesus. They come, in other words, to change our lives, to breach the walls of our small, isolated, private worlds and break us open to ourselves — not because they are better than we are but because they represent experiences, insights, and perspectives which we ourselves have never known and without which, therefore, we would be shallower people. But there is a proviso. Resident in the idea that others have the capacity to stretch the horizons of my soul lies the assumption that there is something in me that makes the evolution possible. I have to be touchable in order to be touched.

In order to create a feminist environment, then, questions have got to be in vogue. Nothing can be off limits to discussion, to exploration, to possibility. Questions are not an indication of chaos; they are an indication of concern. They measure the degree of interest a person brings to a subject. They alert us to significance. Brainstorming, a technique developed in communication theory in the sixties to generate and evaluate ideas in what had been otherwise relatively controlled circumstances, made discussion a safe environment for both the timid and the creative. [82] No idea should be discarded, the theorists suggested, until every idea that had been raised in the group — regardless of its apparent worth and possibility — had been listed and discussed. Nothing was to be automatically dismissed from consideration because it appeared at first to be impossible. Life, in this model, lists more toward the dynamic than the static, more toward the creative than the conservative.

Questions, then, become key to the development of an open mind because a question opens a floodgate of possible answers. The givens of the past maintain a convincing ring and the right to consideration only as long as what they were meant to do they continue to do in the light of present circumstances and current data. To question present assumptions requires faith in the God of the future as well as respect for the God of the past. Somewhere an anonymous philosopher wrote, "Yesterday is history; tomorrow is mystery. Today is God's gift. That's why we call it 'the present.'"

Feminism confronts the world with openness to differences and values them. The stranger becomes the bearer of a new kind of competency, another kind of effectiveness, a treasure house of possibility. Feminism challenges the world to trust again.

The ramifications of trust for the bonding of peoples and the collaboration of groups are legion. Fear of the other melts. Colors fade into one: human. Hierarchies shrink down to size. Differences become gift. Feminism constitutes the counterpoint to authoritarian control. Instead of blocking the emergence of new ideas, new answers, new models to old questions and new problems, feminism unleashes ideas and encourages persons and enables new processes to be judged on merit rather than on fear. Feminism is not chaos gone mad; feminism is creativity gone to the Spirit. The feminist understands the need for order and system, but the feminist does not worship either.

Feminism calls for a world in process. Authoritarianism celebrates the static in life. But people, unique, creative, in process, are anything but static. They are the flow of God through time. To control the Spirit in a person is to run the risk of missing the Spirit ourselves.

Judgment does not come easily to a feminist, nor punishment for differences, nor ostracism for failure, nor limitation by definitions. The infidelity of David, the skepticism of Noah, the gullibility of Adam and Eve, the anger of Jeremiah all point to a God who believes in the spirituality of beginning again. Tolerance for the ambitious apostles, James and John, support of tax collectors, patience with Pharisees, acceptance of Samaritans, and violations of the Sabbath in behalf of the needy all point to a Jesus who made openness a rule of life. The counting of heretics, the judgment of sinners, the feminist leaves to the God of life who gave humankind the gift of life for the purpose of the living of it, learning from it. Life, to a feminist, is an exercise in learning done one hard and faltering step at a time; it is not a series of traps set by a God who tests us by tweaking our tails. Everyone, the feminist knows, deserves the right both to fail in the process and to negotiate it in quantum leaps. Whatever course life takes, for the feminist who welcomes the God of surprises, life is forever a new event, full of mercy, full of promise.

Feminist spirituality emerges from a commitment to consensus rather than control. It assumes the basic value of the individual and depends for its strength on qualities that undermine the patriarchal pyramids in life. Feminists question authority and seek consensus so that authority may be credible and society may be one. The insights of the sincere heart mean more to a feminist than what lies in the charters of patriarchal systems, regardless how ancient, regardless how revered.

Feminist spirituality depends on trust, cooperation, and listening. God, who comes to us in the guise of others, comes seeking acceptance and bringing new truth — theirs — for us to receive, to respect, and to learn from. Closing out anyone closes off truth, yes, but more than that, it closes us off from the power of creation in all its colors, all its chords. The process of reaching back to those who reach out to us binds us to the whole world. The process of reaching out to those who have trouble reaching back identifies us with the God who is love. Listening to those who speak another language than the grammar of our own lives gives us an ear for the God who is truly everywhere.

Feminism brings the beginner's mind to the task of life and allows humankind to begin again, day after day after day.

COMPETITION AND COMPASSION

A NEW GAME OF WINNER GIVES ALL

He was one of the nicest boys I'd ever known. He had a good mind, a fine personality, and wisdom beyond his years. He was one of those rare high-school kids who get known as brains but are liked by both the faculty and the student body, as well. Ted had it all. He came across as smart and normal at the same time and in equal proportions. It was a refreshing combination. He liked to study, and he liked to play, and he did both things with gusto. His father had great plans for him.

I remember the day in the faculty room when I heard the men teachers saying that Ted had gone out for the football team. I blinked. The very thought of it was absurd. In the first place, we were a small school, and boys were in short supply, so he would probably make the squad just by virtue of signing up, but he was far too slight physically for the game. The next smallest boy on the team was twice his weight and half again his height. In the second place, he had told me often as we worked on the school magazine together that he simply didn't like the game. So why in heaven's name was this boy of all boys trying out for a team? He played the piano, competed in speech tournaments, and loved to dance. Why more? And why football of all things?

Night after night I watched him slog down the hall toward the locker room after practice, helmet in hand, wet, tired, and alone. I could see the strain all over his face. "Ted," I said, "why are you doing this? It's clearly not fun for you."

"My dad says I should," he said slowly. I was incredulous.

"Your dad says you have to?" I said. "Whatever for?"

"Because," the boy said, his jaw quivering a bit, "he says that football will make a man out of me."

It was a long, long season for Ted. He went to every practice, suited up for every game, and never played a minute all year long. I couldn't help wondering what kind of a man competition made of him that compassion would not have made. I couldn't help wondering as time went by what kind of man it really made of him in the end.

The United States abounds in groups designed to bring heart to the system. There are hospices for AIDS patients, shelters for the homeless, day-care centers for low-income families, soup kitchens for the hungry, free clinics for the sick, educational opportunities for the children of the inner city. Most of these projects begin in the private sector of the country, many of them begun by women, all of them by people who realize that, from those who have received the goods of the earth, some giving is also expected.

The unspoken law of life shines here. The God who provides for us obliges us, then, to provide for others. We are, indeed, the other's keeper. We are the makers of the human community, the solder of the human family, the proof of the human enterprise. We are charged with taking the raw material of creation and turning it into the human experiment at its most divine or bartering the quality of our own humanity in the process. It is an undertaking markedly in tension with the patriarchal culture that undergirds the bulk of society.

The patriarchal mindset teaches that the purpose of life is to get to the top and hold the territory for fear of invasion. Being tough, being hard, being the best become the qualities that dominate the scale of human values in systems where the spoils go to the strong. The feminist mindset, on the other hand, assumes that the test of humanity lies in making sure that all the paths in life are open and that no one gets left behind in the process of the climb. A patriarchal society assumes the survival of the fittest. A feminist society insists on the survival of all and questions the very definition of what constitutes fitness. Is the paraplegic with the fine mind fit or not? Is the hydrocephalic with the gentle personality fit or not? Was the well-developing fetus never brought to birth fit or not? It is a matter of perspective, a matter of values, that decides which mountains are worth climbing and which qualities are worth preserving if human society is to be human at all.

Programs designed to respond to the real needs of real people rather than to the policy problems of an amorphous people are normally small and always inadequate. They involve a particular response to the human needs that industry and government, business and finance, political parties and social clubs either ignore or do not see or fund in meager proportion. They carry compassion to its necessary end, beyond sympathy, above empathy, to immersion in the suffering itself. Isolated citizens fight back the flood of poverty and pain that threatens to spill over the dikes of affluent North America and seep into cities here as it has in most of the rest of the world.

Churches pray for the poor and sponsor projects designed to alleviate the suffering that comes from need, but the legislation gets more begrudging by the day while the number of children who go to bed hungry every night gets larger by the day. Despite the rising number of working poor in North America — those millions of people who do full-time work for part-time pay or work two jobs a day for less than one full-time salary — companies continue to hire part-time workers to avoid having to pay the compensation and benefits required for full-time employees. Lawmakers cut back on welfare payments in order to force people to work and then blame working mothers for the deteriorating state of child development. The question is: How can it be that this country always has money for guns but regrets money spent for the general good? How is it that when the United States balances the needs of working mothers against the needs of the Pentagon in the great budget contest every election year, the budget deficit always gets blamed on the mothers? The country talks the principles of compassion but functions according to the principles of competition. It is good patriarchy but poor feminism, good capitalism but poor Christianity.

The images of Jesus are, by contemporary standards at least, soft ones. We remember Jesus with children, Jesus with the sick, Jesus with women, Jesus writing forgiveness in the sand, Jesus listening to beggars on the side of the road, Jesus giving over his life to his enemies without a struggle, Jesus, to the end, taking in criminals and outcasts, healing and helping, caring and curing what he can. Jesus fails on patriarchal standards over and over again. Over and over again, he does what is good for the other, regardless of the cost to himself. Over and over again, he gives of himself — his time, his energy, his attention, his personal gifts — to provide for the needs of others. The model is a stark one in a society in which political promises to do less rather than more for the needy attract voter support and political promises to do more lose elections. Jesus is clearly calling all of us — men and women alike — beyond patriarchy. "Come, follow me" begins to take on the ring of a society that compassionates with losers, forgives the unforgivable, rescues the wounded, gives with largesse and makes investments with little hope of interest. A society such as this does not question why there are so few who are so rich; a society such as this questions why there are so many who are so poor. It is a serious and fundamental question, one which, if not resolved, threatens, eventually, not only the weak but the secure themselves. As the inner cities bleed, the suburbs buy more burglar alarms. As the inner city deteriorates, so does the city school system. As the inner cities crumble, the prison population doubles. No one part of any society withers without affecting the other parts. The results are plain to see.

The history of contemporary society in the last seventy-five years emerges out of one unending string of bitter struggles: a labor movement organizing to demand a living wage, women carted off to jail for wanting the right to at least cast a vote for the men who would rule their lives, blacks in search of public water fountains, the handicapped struggling for access to buildings and busses and sidewalks and toilets. It is not a pretty picture in nations such as the United States and Canada that see themselves as messianic, as enlightened, as Christian. There is something missing somewhere. There is an intangible lacking. There is a level of humanity gone astray when those in need of the other human rights — the right to food, the right to shelter, the right to work, the right to a living wage — become the enemy. The question is: What is missing and why?

Access to a great deal of land with only the needs of a small population to satisfy — the paradigm of Western history — makes for two characteristics in the human psyche: a high degree of independence and wide berth for individualism. As the amount of available land on the planet decreases, however, and the size of the human population increases, two other qualities vie for priority. One is competitiveness, and the other is the need for compassion, the claim to community. With resources becoming more and more limited, the two are locked in mortal battle. Patriarchy argues for competitiveness and calls it fair; feminism calls for the common good and calls it justice.

Competition fuels a false sense of right. Those who outrun, defeat, outmaneuver, or outsmart the thousands of others running the same race stake a claim to the prize on the basis of skill or industry or intelligence, as if any one quality can possible justify the loss of essential resources to everybody else. "I won it fair and square," "I paid for it," "I got there first," "I can't help it if they weren't smart enough to figure it out," "I fought them for it and won" are all unacceptable reasons for controlling the resources that other people need to live.

The training in self-reliance, in power games, starts early. Play becomes the method of choice in the Western world's tutelage for dominance. Children learn young to achieve, to compete, to win. Play theorists look closely at the preparation for power built into children's sports, games, and activities and recognize its relationship to life in a society where rugged individualism is a virtue rather than a vice. [83] No doubt about it, in a culture such as this children go on being intimidated into going out for football teams in order to become men when they should be playing the piano in order to become human beings. There is a great deal to be learned here that has nothing to do with the game. It is gaming that is important, winning that is paramount, personal hardening that is its purpose. No softness here, no give here, no compassion here. Just winning. Just trophies. Just patriarchy.

In a competitive culture, work becomes an instrument of control. People do not work to co-create; they work to get ahead. Work itself becomes an exercise in winning more money, more status, more power. It is a sad and sterile existence, this use of the earth for our own aggrandizement alone, far from the theology of the Garden, far from the generativity that Genesis demands of us.

Work in the feminist worldview brings compassion to action. What we do reflects what we are. Compassion moves beyond words of pity to works for change. The suffering I see in front of me is not there as a spur to reflection, one more boring occasion in life for the intellectualization of issues. It is there as my goad to conversion. The world I live in, not the perfume of incense and the sweet words of prayer, is the stuff of my sanctification. To ignore the suffering around me in the name of being realistic or reasonable or objective about it — as women are repeatedly told to be — makes me culpable not simply of the situation itself but of what scholastic theologians call "giving full consent of the will." I see it, I think about it, I consider it, and I decide to do nothing about it at all. I am too busy. It is too large a problem for one person to do anything about. The people involved are too questionable. Or, most commonly, it's not my responsibility. Compassion says, yes, it is.

Work carries the gift of compassion to the world at large. We work, compassion says, to make the world a better place for everyone. Work is about more than survival, more than profit. The continuing creation of the globe depends on the kind of work we do, the quality of work we do, the character of the work we do. Doing work that rapes the land or threatens the globe or denies the worker a living wage corrupts compassion at its root.

But what we do is only half the value of our work; how we do it is equally important. Quality, too, determines the impact of work on the nature of life. Cleaning ladies who clean corners with hot, sudsy water, clerks who keep records in readable script, teachers who grade papers one sentence at a time leave great, gaping holes in the world when they go. With them, the world runs well, people thrive, the future comes with certainty. Without them, the world is a less kindly place to grow in, a less wholesome place to be. Those who work with real compassion serve soup in sparkling-clean soup kitchens and cover garbage cans in apartment buildings and make callbacks in offices. They do whatever they do with dignity and care. They give real service. They go to work to make their corner of the world a better place to be because the rest of the world deserves that kind of respect; they don't go to work simply to collect a paycheck. Compassion requires us to realize that whatever we do well makes life a little better for everyone around us.

We work to discover ourselves, our little impatiences, the breadth of our hearts, the depth of our secret needs, the limits of our strengths, so that, becoming everything we can be in life, we can become the gift of compassion to those around us. Once we come to know and accept ourselves as lacking, we become capable of understanding others. Once we realize our own emptiness, we can accept the needs of others. Once we face the fact that there is something missing in us, we can look to the other as equal, as needy as we are, as human. Then we have the raw material of equality. It is not compassion that scatters alms from above the fray in handfuls to screaming crowds below. That kind of display is spiritual playacting. Compassion comes from a sense of solidarity with the human race, of knowing what someone needs because we have needed it, too. Compassion is what we learn at the first funeral we attend after the funeral of the person we ourselves loved most in life. Once we ourselves suffer loss, we come to understand what loss does to others. And to suffer with it.

The work we do teaches us both our strengths and our shortcomings. The spirituality of a patriarchal system demands the pursuit of perfection. But feminist spirituality knows that it is precisely perfection that can become the most insidious of virtues. What we fail to do becomes as important in our search for compassion as what we do well. Perfectionism denies a person's humanity and leaves small room for compassion for those who do not meet our standards. The mystic Julian of Norwich warns us well. "Sin is behoovable," Julian tells us. Sin is, in other words, necessary to our understanding of ourselves. Sin teaches us that life is a process of growth, not a state of perfection. Sin brings us face to face with ourselves and saves us from the terminal illness of arrogance, an affliction that cuts us off from the rest of the human race and leaves us bereft of compassion for others.

We work to develop our gifts. We work to fulfill creation. We work to provide for the poor. We work to become like God, bountiful and improvident in love. Compassion and work go hand in hand. Together they have the potential to turn the world upside-down.

When competition corrodes the spiritual value of work, compassion dies, and in its stead lies the search for achievement, the drive to power, the stroking of the ego. It is a sad excuse for the spending of the self on the co-creation of the globe.

Competition and compassion are values in tension. One is patriarchal; one is feminist. One appropriates the world unto itself; the other gives the self away in behalf of the development of the other and in the process becomes more whole itself. Competition depends on losers. Compassion makes winners of us all.

VULNERABILITY AND STRENGTH

A NEW PARADOX

It was one of those university weekend-workshop situations where I would meet a group Friday night, work with them all day Saturday, and close the session before noon on Sunday. It was a heavy schedule for all of us, but the idea was to leave the members of the course with enough material for them to process together on their own after I left. These people would be together for the rest of the semester. What they learned about the effects of sexism on both men and women would affect their relationships together for weeks to come.

That day I had gone back to the classroom early after lunch to lay out the papers and overheads for the Saturday-afternoon session. I could see someone waiting at the conference-room door at the far end of the hallway, plastic bag in hand, as I arrived. He was a huge, hairy fellow with torn-off shorts, a big barrel chest, and a T-shirt just small enough to prove it. "Frankie, didn't you go to lunch?" I asked him when I got to the doorway.

"I picked up a sandwich," he said and then went rushing on before I could ruin the day with more small talk. "I wanted to come back early because I need to ask you something," he said. Oh, oh, I thought, here it comes: the women-should-be-women argument.

"Sure, anything," I said. "What do you want to know?" He raised the shopping bag up in front of me.

"First, open this," he said. The bag was lighter than I had expected.

"What is it?" I said. There was something curled up on a rod inside it and wrapped in an outer layer of plastic.

"Take it out; look at it," he said. I realized that he was watching me, hard. He was searching every muscle in my face. I moved to a desk, put my own briefcase down, and cleared an area where I could unroll the material on the rod to the full.

"Frankie, this is gorgeous," I said. The piece of needlepoint, half-finished, was a medieval pattern, the kind that hung on castle walls, tight and bright and intricate. "Wherever did you get it?" I asked him.

"I made it," he said.

"You made it?" I said with an incredulity in my voice that I have regretted ever since. "Where did you learn to do such things?"

"My grandmother taught me when I was nine years old," he said. "I've been doing it ever since." He paused for a second. "But no one — no one — knows." He looked hard at me again. "After what you said this morning, I began to think about things. I decided that I don't want to hide anymore. But I need your help. I'm afraid to do this," he said, and I saw the mist settle over his eyes.

"What are you afraid of, and what can I do to help you?" I said softly, beginning to feel a little misty-eyed myself.

"I want to sit in the front seat and work on this hanging while you teach," the huge boy-man said. "You see, if you're talking about this stuff while I'm working, maybe nobody will laugh."

Believe me, I learned a great deal more that day than I taught.

Under all the pomp and steel, despite all the money and guns, beyond all the status and roles, the world, we all know down deep, is a very vulnerable place. Nothing stands completely safe from the exigencies of living, the dailiness of survival, the fragility of life even at its most benign. Whatever our securities, the sense of nakedness, of alert, of potential danger never leaves us. We are vulnerable from all sides, in and out, up and down, past, present, and future. We fear vulnerability. It takes a great deal of living to discover that, actually, vulnerability comes to us more as friend than as enemy. Vulnerability may be the greatest strength we have.

Vulnerability bonds us to one another and makes us a community in league with life. Because we need one another, we live looking for good in others, without which we ourselves can not survive, will not grow, can not become what we ourselves have the potential to be. Vulnerability is the gift given to us to enable us to embed ourselves in the universe.

We are born dependent and spend the rest of our lives coming to wholeness. It is a delicate and dangerous process, requiring an untold amount of support and an amazing degree of forgiveness as we stumble and grope our way from one new part of life to another. Vulnerability, in fact, is the one hallmark of life which, try as we might, we can not cure.

Vulnerability, therefore, is clearly part of the spiritual process, clearly part of the human endeavor. To know ourselves to be exposed to forces outside ourselves, beyond our control, teaches us the power of both darkness and light, gives us gifts from the depths of the unknown, introduces us to the mystery of life. Because we are defenseless, we can't possibly close ourselves off from the rest of the world. We can't escape into self. We can't be self-sufficient. We are put in a position where we have no choice but to go out of ourselves to others in order to draw from them what we ourselves would otherwise be left without. We come to see the holiness around us, and, God willing, we have the sense to learn from it. Vulnerability gives us the gift of our own limitations, and from the darkness of despair we learn to trust in the gifts of those who are seeking our own giftedness in return. Vulnerability turns the potential for narcissism into the commitment to community. What we would least be inclined to trust in life, we find ourselves dependent on, and then, thrown upon the unknown, we come face to face with life the creator. Vulnerability saves us from ourselves and, as a result, makes us more than, without it, we could ever be. It taps every fear, every feeling, every ounce of heart we have. It ties us to the human condition. It makes us feeling people. Because we know ourselves to be vulnerable, we know ourselves to be human — full of humility, full of love, full of hope. It is the stuff of great spiritual insight, deep spiritual experience, and boundless spiritual bonding. Nothing is more valuable to human development than a vulnerability that opens us to the world. Nothing is more indicative of spiritual depth than a vulnerability that counts weakness as the opportunity to learn from the model of those before us.

At the same time, nothing is more reprehensible to a patriarchal world than the weakness of those who own their own limitations without shame and suffer unashamedly for the oppression of others, as well. Such types are not tolerated easily. The culture has, on the contrary, devoted itself instead to the crafting of personalities in whom weakness, the acknowledgment of feeling, and the display of emotion had little or no part.

Emotional strength, in fact, ranked as the hallmark of the eighteenth century's aspiring middle class. Social scientists document that emotional control became one of the distinguishing criteria separating the newly emerging commercial class from its lower-class counterparts. [84] Balance, the emerging social consciousness held, was not simply a nicety practiced by Boston Brahmins. It was not simply the price of the ticket to be paid for the crossing of economic boundaries between those born to the manor and those newly established. It was much more than that. It was, at the same time, in fact, the scientific basis for both physical and mental health. Constraint, eighteenth-century professionals agreed, involved more than emulation of social conventions. On the contrary. In this culture, emotional control had something to do with actual physical survival. Medical records derived from the period of the yellow-fever epidemic in eighteenth-century Philadelphia make plain the then-current connection between emotional responses and physical health. Researchers document that popularizers of scientific medicine of the period "warned their readers repeatedly that failing to moderate one's passions, particularly the emotions of anger, fear, grief, pride, greed, and even love and joy, would result in illness, madness, and quite possibly death." [85] What life demanded was balance, moderation, calm, repression, or "uncommon tranquility of mind," as one doctor called it in explaining his own survival in the midst of a sea of dying patients.

Fear, in particular, was the emotion marked out for special treatment in this milieu. Without the eradication of fear, many said, the infection was certain to spread. Fear itself generated susceptibility to the disease. Stories of death due to fear were everywhere. Men told of leaving the bedrooms of wives who confessed their fear of the epidemic. They left, these men reported, not to avoid contracting the disease but to avoid contracting the fear of it. Emotion, in other words, weakened the body's resistance to disease.

But if fear was debilitating, strength — emotional distance from danger — constituted an obdurate defense against it. Being strong, being fearless, became a medical prescription, a social norm. As a result, little by little, the bias for rigid personality formation gave way to the even more exacting standards of modern medicine. Fear became aberrant, unacceptable, detestable. Strength became the scale against which human development was graded. Strength, in the sense of emotional reserve, became standardized, idealized. And decidedly male. *Strong* became a synonym for *emotional repression*. To be without feelings was to be strong.

Women, the theoreticians of the period argued, had the seeming potential for emotional control — a nod to the essentially distinguishing mark of the entire species — but could never really achieve it. Since their nervous systems were more delicate physically than those of men, their natural sensibilities more susceptible generally, and their will weaker to begin with, though men had the natural capacity to fashion the environment, women could only suffer it. [86] The stage was set. Science had spoken: Women's emotions, like their bodies, were genderized. To Freud and his followers, women were hysterics. To theologians in the tradition of Thomas Aquinas, Luther, and Calvin, women were derivative and therefore diminished human beings from the start. To Hegel and other philosophers, women were means to an end in the construction of the patriarchal society. The question was closed.

Few, if any, challenged the definition of terms itself. Who said that to be strong meant to be without emotional response? Who said that human responses to inhuman situations are weakness? Who benefited from the explanations that were being given? Is strength really the ability to cut myself off from the world around me? Or is strength the ability to open myself to the world and then to cope with what I find there? Is it possible that strength may really be the ability to have the character to cry in the face of suffering? And what are the implications for spirituality of both positions?

The synapse between reason, religion, and science worked effectively to enthrone strength, self-control, self-containment, as the acme of human development and to disparage vulnerability, the recognition of emotional connectedness, as an essentially healthy aspect of life. Instead, sensitivity became the enemy, emotional distance the measure of adulthood. In this scenario, John Wayne and Humphrey Bogart, Mike Tyson and Oliver North become models of manhood, and manhood becomes the model of human control. More than that, spirituality itself becomes a dry and sense-less thing when weakness is rejected and self-absorption espoused as models of the spiritual life.

This is a spirituality that teaches an astringent existence. This view of human nature generates a spirituality that teaches control but not expression. From this perspective, saintliness comes to depend more on what a person does not do than on what a person does. The whole notion of living life to the hilt, of finding as much holiness in the expression of joy as in its repression, gets short shrift in an environment that takes inhibition as a fact of life.

At first blush, the effects of such a worldview seem minimal at worst. A closer analysis, however, indicates the degree to which such a contortion of human values touches every aspect of life. Personal development itself is warped. Relationships suffer. The world becomes an object rather than a lifeline to the universe.

The socialization of men and women draws heavily on a definition of strength that makes men unfeeling and women uncontrolled. Little boys are taught not to cry. Little girls are allowed to cry and then devalued because they do so. Boys are ridiculed for being less than self-sufficient. Girls face control at all times, amiably protective or brutally restrictive. Neither child — boy or girl — in other words, has the luxury of becoming a full adult with the full range of responses that such development implies. Boys, men, are given the right to anger; women, the right to depression. The results, of course, are populations that value football and bullfighting, war and discipline and derogate shelters for the homeless, universal health care, and hospices for battered women. This is a society of rugged individualists who see vulnerability as weakness and insensitivity as strength.

The social cost of such personality formation is only coming into focus. Social psychologists, attempting to determine the underlying rationale behind the growing phenomenon of sexually aggressive men, find three clear strains of emotional repression in them. Men who attack women reject anything labeled feminine or emotional as weak; they reject anything that violates the male image of strength; they disconnect from whole aspects of their own emotional life. The more men reject feminine attributes, in other words, the more they reject intimacy itself and the emotional connectedness that comes with the development of feminine vulnerability. As a result, they lose their own capacity for empathy. They simply don't feel anything anymore except, of course, rage for those who do. [87]

The ramifications of such bifurcated emotional development bring new insight to the nature of spirituality as it became more and more refined throughout history. Suffering, deprivation, and rigid discipline have been its stock in trade. Hildegard of Bingen, Teresa of Avila, Julian of Norwich, Meister Eckhart, Benedict of Nursia, Francis of Assisi, Martin Luther, and Rumi provide a refreshing strain of normalcy and joy in the spiritual life, but they are rare figures in a catechism of rigorists. What's more, their lives get quickly reinterpreted to meet the demands of a culture that defined development as the ability to develop only partially. Like Abraham on Horeb, the sacrifice of Isaac, the destruction of the self, becomes an acceptable, even holy, response to a God we do not know well enough to realize that the God of creation would never ask such a thing.

Endurance, fortitude, and sufferance became the center of the spiritual life, not joy, not holy abandon, not the carnival of goodness everywhere. Gone was access to the beauty of the Garden, and in its place emerged the fear of the serpent. Gone was the wedding feast at Cana, and in its place, Golgotha alone. So much for the Jesus who went fishing with friends, celebrated with Pharisees, cried over the dead, fled from the crowds, loved both women and men, and struggled with depression in deserts and gardens. Life in the world of the strong reeks of immaturity, of incompleteness.

Suppression of emotion on the personal level and expression of emotion on the liturgical level provide a kind of schizophrenic model of human life. The message seems to be that personal emotional expression is bad but that formalized emotional participation is necessary. Life in this gear becomes an exercise in personal repression of stultifying proportion, a robo-tizing of public participation. We learn in the process to hide our real selves in order to become a public self that goes through the motions of feeling unfeelingly. We learn to spiritualize, to ritualize, and to deny the depth of feelings, the vulnerability to life, that is the raw material of both our humanity and our sanctification.

The cost to relationships between men and women looms larger with each passing day. Women have permission to approach the world with guards down and hearts open, provided they are willing to barter public respect for the right to be human. Men get strong subterranean messages to regard life as an endurance test, a mountain, a possible trap, a struggle to be won, a mask to be worn for fear of signaling weakness to a predator world. Most of all, they know not to trust themselves to it. Men take it for granted that their role is to shape the world to themselves. Women take it for grant-ed that they will be shaped by it. The results of the two distinct perspectives show everywhere: in social attitudes, in public activities, in personal rela-tionships, in the spiritual life itself.

Thanks to patriarchal valuing of strength over vulnerability — the Greek dictate that a man come back from the battlefields of life "carrying his shield or on it" — we can still, at the beginning of the second millenni-um, make as a criterion for the presidency of the United States the concern that the candidate must be strong enough to press the nuclear button that would annihilate the world. We never ask whether a candidate is strong enough *not* to press the nuclear button.

As a result of the adulation of strength over vulnerability, we disregard the social needs of women for the traditional needs of men. We now allow women to do more things that were traditionally the province only of men, but we do not take these things seriously when women do them. Women's sports take second place on school schedules. Women's agendas take second place on legislative agendas. The overall comparison of women to men is still based more on physical data than on mental equivalence in a culture that is less physical and more technological every day — and despite the fact that tests even of physical capacity indicate that women, on the basis of armed-forces standards, are at least proportionally as strong as men in all areas and stronger than men in some. Women are not essentially weak, in other words. They are proportionally weak — as any small man would be weaker than most large men — or highly underdeveloped because develop-ing women physically has not been a hallmark of modern culture. Strength belonged to men, both physical and emotional. Women have paid the price for that lack of development, often with their very lives — intellectually, emotionally, and even physically.

As serious as the distinctions have been on the public and social level, however, the definition of strength as emotional restraint has been most detrimental of all, perhaps, at the level of interpersonal relations. Feminist men know the price of having been emotionally suffocated in their public lives. Macho men have too often paid the price in their personal relations. Women have paid it in barren lives lived without emotional companionship or in emotional hinterlands where intimacy has no heart.

The fact is that intimacy thrives only on vulnerability. It requires self-disclosure and assumes the kind of equality that makes the mutual normal.[88] No power plays here. No hierarchy here. No diminishment here. Just the wonder of being known at every level and being honest at every juncture and being open at every moment. Intimacy is precisely what links us to the other who makes us whole. Relationships — marriages — built on roles leave little room for that baring of mind, that unity of heart, that becomes the meeting place of the world in a microcosm of two. When men are taught to be strong and unresponsive and women are taught that they are by virtue of their responsiveness weak, neither can fully trust themselves or the other. Then friendship turns into adolescent companionship; then love turns into prostitution and exploitation rather than mutuality and self-giving; then marriage turns into a power struggle marked by violent demands and passive aggression to right the balance that can never be righted in a world that endows him with domination and curses her with self-abnegation.

Intimacy requires exactly what the patriarchal definition of strength refuses to recognize and is loath to allow, the confession of feelings beyond my control. Intimacy implies the total exposure of me and all my weaknesses to the one who can handle them reverently and love them all to life. There is no forfeiture of self like the surrender that comes with the trust of another. It is the laying down of arrogance, of self-sufficiency, of autonomy, of power. It is a coming out of hiding that makes me vulnerable for the rest of my life. It opens me to abandon and allies me with all the weak and wounded of the world. However it comes, there is nothing like it to help me take the measure of myself, to grow to full stature, to find mystery in the commonplace, and to retire forever from my attempts to be God.

A spirituality of strength comes out of the patriarchal mind for the sake of the patriarchy. A spirituality of vulnerability arises from a feminist sense of union with a gentle, gifting universe and the experience of finally coming home to it with trust and hope.

The Patriarchal Woman

INTERNALIZED OPPRESSION

The writing started when I was still a child. I remember writing stories in grade school about imaginary brothers. In high school I worked on the school newspaper day and night. After I entered the convent, I discovered the spiritual journal, probably provoked by Merton's Sign of Jonas, which was very popular at the time. Whatever the cause, the fact was that I simply could not not write. I recorded every thought I had about the spiritual life, every reaction I had to the newness of monastic life, every response I had to the structures of formation and the nature of community life. I worked on the journal every night in the novitiate just before lights out and then tucked it into the corner of my tiny desk only to begin again on every day that followed. I knew, somehow, that someday I would look back on this work as a treasure house of idea development, a map of my own spiritual coming of age.

One morning I went to my novitiate desk to add a paragraph as usual and discovered that the journal was missing. It was not under the spiritual-reading book on the right side of the old drop-top desk. It was not under the stationery on the left side either. The desk was the only private place a novice had except for a three-drawer clothes stand by the bed. The journal had to be in the desk. There was nowhere else it could be.

Our novice mistress was a rigid woman who lived by the book. Her role, she thought, was to turn us all into what the male world said were good nuns. She scrutinized our cleaning assignments with exhausting precision, she kept us to rigid schedules, she demanded unquestioning conformity, she emphasized unfailing obedience, and she punished infractions swiftly. I watched her closely from the day the journal showed up missing, but, harsh as she was with us, much as I found myself on my knees in front of her, often for less than perfect adherence to the rules, I never saw so much as a glimmer of indication from her that she was even aware of the journal, let alone in possession of it. Nevertheless, down deep in me I knew there was no other explanation. She had to have it; she surely had it. I was puzzled. And wary. Difficult as it was to stop the flow of reflections in me, I never wrote another personal word in all those years.

Five years later, the night before my final profession, I got word that the novice mistress wanted me to meet her down the hall from the scholasticate, at the elevator. It was a strange request. We had hardly seen one another in years and never ever talked about anything when we did. Night Silence had, in fact, already begun. No one talks about anything to anyone after night prayer in a monastery. Nevertheless, she was indeed waiting for me, elevator at the ready, when I came down the hall. Silently and solemnly she took me to the basement, then to the boiler room, and finally to the incinerator. "Open it," she whispered as she brought something out from under her apron. I recognized it instantly. My journal. "Here," she said as I swung open the top of the flaming furnace. "I think you ought to burn this now. You don't want to do this kind of thing anymore."

But why not? I thought as I threw the journal slowly and reluctantly into the fire. To this day, I can see the flames curling around those pages still. The only difference is that now I know the answer to the question.

Spirituality demands that people turn belief into the stuff of everyday existence. Theology is a system of thought, but spirituality is the response that wells up in the human heart in the face of eternal truth. To be a truly spiritual person implies that we live a life that looks in the daytime the way it reads in the books. We know, for instance, that human beings have free will and reason and feelings and minds and hearts. We know that life is given to us in order for us to develop all of those to the height of their promise. We know that we are the raw material of divine hope. We know, each of us, that our task in life is to become everything we can possibly be. We know that life is a gift but that wholeness is an obligation. We know that we have within us everything it takes, everything we need, to become truly human, fully human, beautifully human. And we also know that many people go to their graves never having become half of what they could have been, given other circumstances, given other theology, given other theory.

Life can only be lived one person at a time. We may talk about it in generalities, but it is lived one experience at a time and singly, not in groups. No one else can live life for us. No one else can make our mistakes or develop our gifts or waste our time. At least theoretically. But theory is just theory, however, an idea that seems to explain something but which falters at the plane of the absolute, that fails at the level of the actual. This particular theory of personal freedom, for instance, sounds very nice. The problem is that it doesn't always follow so neatly that individuals really feel free to become what they really want to become. Though every human being alive has the essential ability to make independent decisions, decisions are not made out of clouds and stardust. They form out of the matter of our lives. Breaking through invisible barriers, stepping out of plexiglass boxes of cultural conventions to become ourselves when we have never really been allowed to be ourselves, challenges personal courage and culture to the core. There are things outside ourselves that limit us, that hold us back, that restrict us. There are, we know, expectations to be dealt with. There are standards to be kept. There are obligations to be met. But whose?

The great social question of our time is not only what is appropriate for whom, but who decides what is appropriate and on the basis of what criteria? Who decides what a woman is, what a man is, what a person is? The great spiritual question of our time seeps out of the same crack, emerges from the same source, derives from the same confusion: What happens to the souls of those who have no part in determining the standards and conventions and roles that govern their lives and take their freedom and leave them more or less whole, more or less real? Why, indeed, do we burn the journals of our private selves to become selves defined by someone else? And what self is it that we finally become, our own or someone else's?

The question rankles, but it is an important one, nevertheless. How do we account, for instance, for the woman who accepts the patriarchal definition of the world and limits herself to its roles, honors its prescriptions, agrees with its tenets, and claims as loudly as or louder than any man, "If a woman wears revealing clothing and is raped, it's her own fault," or, "When women are ordained, the image of Jesus will be lost," or, "If women work, they are still responsible for the homemaking chores"? How is it that women themselves come to diminish what it is to be a woman? How is it that women accuse God of having made them less competent, less creative human beings than men — who are made of the same human fabric as they themselves are — when they know that God says otherwise in Genesis and acts otherwise in Jesus? What is the price of that kind of bifurcated thinking for spiritual development? And what is the price to spirituality of becoming feminist in a patriarchal society, as well?

Decade after decade now, another group of voiceless, faceless, forgotten people arise to claim their birthright from a system that has banished them to its bottom, kept them on its edge, shunted them out of consciousness, and treated them as nonpersons. First blacks, then Indians, then women, then gays began to insist on being admitted to the conference halls and parliaments and research centers of humanity. Everywhere around the globe the little people of the world — half the human race, all of Africa, most of the minorities of the world, laborers of every nation, the handicapped, the battered, and the beggared — have begun to stake their ownership to life full and free. The process has not been easy. At first the voices were timid; at first the clamors were more requests, pleas, beggars' cries for help than they were demands for justice. At first the disadvantaged of the patriarchal world, the ones who could not compete, who were not empowered politically, who had been on the bottom of the pyramid all their lives, began to question. Then, conquered, disenfranchised, enslaved, or impoverished, they discovered that they had nothing left to lose but themselves in remaining silent.

Invariably, part of the process involves bringing the oppressed themselves to a sense of their own situation, their entitlement as human beings, their right to justice. "Conscientization," the liberation theologians called it. "Social sin," the moralists called it. "Internalized oppression," the social scientists called it. "Worthlessness," the oppressed call it. The oppressed had been well taught.

People come to know who they are by virtue of what other people tell them they are. [89] The fact is that self-image is largely a social construct. People defined as unworthy by a society come to define themselves as unworthy. People learn that they are slow or shy or pretty or smart because other people, significant people — their parents, their teachers, their heroes — tell them that they are. The way we view the other, in other words, has a great deal to do with the way they come to view themselves. The implications of these findings have serious consequences for women as well as for any other minority in any society.

Prejudice studies indicate that oppressed people deal with the effects of prejudice in four ways. First, they become what the dominant class defines them to be. Second, they live down to the stunted expectations their society has of them. Third, they seek the approval of the oppressor. Fourth, they turn their anger at the situation inward on themselves rather than outward on the oppressor. [90] The results of such a situation shrink and shrivel the souls of everybody concerned.

The situation is clear: Women become what men want them to be. They wear what men want them to wear, do what men want them to do, think what men say they should think. Women know from every theology book they ever read, every survey-of-philosophy course they ever took, every psychological study conducted before 1970 that they are weak, inferior, and intellectually deficient. By nature. They learn to doubt their own judgments, their own insights, their own instincts, their own abilities not less, but more and more as they get older. They become, with a few outstanding exceptions, exactly what the patriarchal world has defined them to be: its helpers, its servants, its handmaidens in every field.

Whatever women, in the innocence and excitement of childhood, aspire to has been carefully culled across time. Women learn young to live down to the stunted expectations imposed on them by the society around them. They were taught that they could be cook but not chef, nurse but not doctor, teller but not manager of the bank. The patriarchal system told women they could not run marathons, and so women didn't run them. Patriarchal men told women they were too weak to play basketball on the whole court, and women never tried the game. Patriarchal society told women that they could not do math and science, and few women did. Patriarchal society told women that politics was a male preserve, and so women never ran for office. Patriarchal society told women that they were responsible for the sexual responses of men, so mothers dutifully taught their daughters whose fault rape really was. No wonder it is women who say that women can't be president, can't be priests, can't be airline pilots, can't be the primary wage earner in the family. Or worse, no wonder it is women who reject women who are.

Oppressed peoples, ironically, look to the oppressor for their standard of achievement and measure of approval. Blacks straightened their hair and lightened their skin before they discovered a black beauty independent of white culture. Women find themselves locked into male academic models, male corporate uniforms, male structures, and male models of the world's major institutions, all designed to facilitate a world designed from the perspective of men for the convenience and comfort of men. To succeed in this world, women conform to norms they never had a chance to help create. The archetype of female achievement lies in becoming like men at the male game. Being approved by men as one of the team, a good nun, the perfect wife, a good Christian, a real scholar, or a good mother marks the highest level of female accomplishment. It's these women who don't want to be thought of as strident feminists for asking for the same compensation for women as for men in the same situation. They want to be nice feminists — if they will use the word at all. It's these women who don't make the changes in family life that would enable their own lives to flower because change would upset their husbands and cost the kind of uneasy peace that is built on their confinement in exchange for his satisfaction. It is these women who want other women to be quiet, to be pleasant, to be grateful for whatever they get, however little it is on the human scale.

In the end, women, like other minorities who have been taught their natural limitations by the dominant culture in which they live, turn their anger against themselves. They come to realize their weakness, their defects, their natural disabilities, and, mistrusting themselves, they mistrust women in general. After that, the conquest is complete. They believe anything that a patriarchal system tells them about themselves, about what God wants for them, about the value of their souls, about the nature of their relationship with God, about the plans that God has for them, about the potential that is theirs to parlay into fullness of life, about the ceiling that God has put on a woman's potential, about the fact that God gave women brains, apparently, so that they could suffer the ache of not being allowed to use them. They know that women can not do what men can do, and they resent and scold and criticize any woman who tries to do it. They become instruments of the system, its perfect product, its most important achievement. Max Weber says that power is most complete when the powerless themselves accept it without question. [91] No doubt about it: Patriarchal power is, for far too many, most complete.

For these women, the price of patriarchy requires the price of personhood. Patriarchal women turn into oppressors of other women, true, but only because they have been victimized themselves. Spiritually, they live without ever knowing the full scope of life, the real extent of their potential, the real depth of their own souls. At the same time, the rest of the world loses the value of their unpursued ministries, the quality of their unrecorded insights, the power of the unsought wisdom in them that is waiting to be tapped like sap from a tree in winter. Most painful of all, perhaps, the daughters of the world never see modeled in these patriarchal women — for their own future use — the resurrection of a soul that, once buried by a patriarchal system, has come to fullness of life.

But there is a price for feminist consciousness, as well.

Feminist men find themselves ridiculed, marginalized, silenced, belittled, often even shunned by a patriarchy that has no place for men who realize that patriarchy is an insufficient response to the gospel, who are open to new ideas, who seek a new worldview, who have a fuller appreciation of God than simply another version of human maleness. Men who respect, need, reach out for the input of women are commonly not welcome in arenas where maleness is defined as total independence, whatever its effect on others. Feminist men find themselves out of touch with both men and women in their attempt to become a new kind of man in a sphere populated largely by women. At the same time, they feel the release that comes with being able to put down the pressures of machoism and the masks of manliness. They find new wholeness in themselves, new freedom to become a full human being, a new way to be with women, and the right to be themselves.

Feminist women, too, find bars and barriers everywhere. Most of all, they find themselves in institutions inimical at the base to feminist ideals. They struggle with marriages built on obedience, in careers built on male power structures, and in churches that preach feminist ideals but operate according to patriarchal principles and in the patriarchal language that erases their very existence. They find themselves with few opportunities to nourish the feminist ideals within them, limited support from the people around them, and negligible resources from which to take direction. Largely alone in the process, they are thrown back time and time again on internal strength that is starved for nourishment and waiting for relief. At the same time, they also find an internal freedom that gives them not the right but the mandate to be what they must be to be whole. Spiritually they grow into new faith, a new image of God, a new sense of call, a vibrant sense of possibility. They grow and give and walk through life beyond the pale shadow of personhood. They come to trust their insights, their strength of soul, their responsibility in the economy of salvation. They move beyond blindness to light, past servanthood to a sainthood based on the resonance of the human soul to the sound of God within it.

To the feminist, women and men are full partners in the human enterprise, not one a potentate and the other a helpmate. Not one the image of God and the other the temptress of the human race. Feminist spirituality bridges the isolation of both women and men and gives both of them a chance finally, finally, to be whole.

The Cosmic Vision of Creation

A CIRCLE, NOT A PYRAMID

The breakfast, lecture, and discussion period of the Culture and Spirituality Conference ended precisely on time. It was a business persons' gathering, and these were people who could not be late for the board meeting, could not delay their arrival at court, could not leave the office unattended first thing in the morning. Nevertheless, a number of people had managed to stay behind to talk. As a result, it was at least another hour before I got downstairs to the car-park door. The two men standing there were obviously waiting for something. It took a moment for me to realize that I was it.

The first man, neatly dressed, impeccably appointed, stepped gently but adroitly in front of me as I circled around them to reach the exit. "I was wondering as you talked if you saw anything good in competition," he said.

"Of course," I said as I turned to face him, "provided that it's just."

"But what's 'just'?" the second man said, stepping forward to insert himself in the conversation. "I mean, they're better off with us than without us, no matter what we do there."

The conversation got intense. Making baseballs on one side of the border for thirty cents each and selling them in the United States for thirteen dollars is not just, I argued. Exporting our jobs but not our medical benefits, our pension plans, our Fair Labor Standards Act, or our wage scale is not just, I went on. "Oh, no. Oh, no. Huh uh," the second man said with a vigorous shake of the head. "We couldn't possibly give them the kind of wage down there that people get up here," he insisted.

"And why not?" I asked in disbelief.

"Because it wouldn't be appropriate to that culture," he shot back with total conviction and deep satisfaction with the truth of his answer.

*I felt my heart drop. What is it about white Western business stan-
dards that can lead to such an opinion? Since when are food on the table,
a house instead of a lean-to hut, education for your children, and clothes
for a child inappropriate to anybody's culture — not to mention the cars,
telephones, and running water that white Westerners take for granted?
How is it that what is appropriate, desirable, necessary for my life and
culture can possibly be seen as inappropriate for someone else's?*

What the world needs are more circles and fewer pyramids. Circles are
strange and wonderful things. No one knows where a circle either begins or
ends. No one can tell what is its most accomplished part. There is no up to
go to in a circle, no steps to climb to arrive there, no top to get to, no crown-
ing point upon which to plant a flag or stake a claim or build a throne. In a
circle there is only eye-to-eye conversation, only shoulder-to-shoulder contact, only community to aspire to rather than hierarchy.

Ladders and pyramids assume a society of serfs, of peasants, of lackeys
and underlings, of in-groups and out-groups, of higher and lower classes.
Circles, on the other hand, assume a society of equals. It isn't that circles
are disorderly or chaotic; it's just that they depend more on consensus than
they do on control. It isn't that circles have no room for leaders; it's just
that they have no respect for despots, no matter how benign. It isn't that
circles lack power; it's simply that circles distribute power and pyramids
amass it at the top.

Pyramids dominate the social patterns of the modern world, true, but
there are living examples of societal circles, as well. Various tribes, some religious traditions, and women as a class consciously organize themselves col-
legially. There are Indian villages in Chiapas, Mexico, for instance that to
this day organize their world on the model of the circle rather than the ladder. Nothing is done in these Indian villages until the entire village agrees
to the plan. It's a slow process but an immensely satisfying one.

Benedictinism, a lifestyle formed in the spirit of the Gospels in the midst
of the patriarchal society of the Roman Empire, is a way of life structured on
communal direction as well. Benedictine communities have functioned in
the design of a circle as a matter of rule for over fifteen hundred years.
"Before anything of importance can be decided," the Rule of Benedict
instructs, "all the members must be called for counsel and the abbot must ask
everyone their opinion, starting with the youngest...." Hundreds of years
before the fall of monarchies or the emergence of philosophies built on the
notion of human rights or the creation of the first democratic societies in the

history of the world, Benedictines modeled a way of life that was nonhierarchical, non-absolutist, non-power oriented.

Women, never part of the power structure, never confronted with ladders to climb, have always functioned extremely well in circles. They gathered in prayer circles and sewing circles and the circle of the family. They functioned without pyramids, without power, without status, without expectation of positions of honor or institutional domination. They learned to function as one human being among many and became totally human because of it. Humanity was, of course, precisely their weakness in a patriarchal society that defined persons by biology rather than soul. Yet, because of women, the entire human race had the chance to be a touch more human as well.

Finally, the earth itself is a circle that has been treated as a pyramid, cut up into pieces, dominated, destroyed, and doomed to struggle for its own existence and the survival of those who depend on it but live under the philosophy of the pyramid. Circles bind the human race together; pyramids separate it into layers of humanity, one level standing on the backs of another.

How can it happen that what warps the human race can become the model of what is expected to empower it? How can it be that an entire population can be seduced, like lemmings on the way to the sea, to organize for its own destruction, to adopt a structure in which some are required to exist for the satisfaction of the others, in which most are exploited and many are destroyed for the sake of the few? What is it that fuels planetary suicide, that separates women and men, and warps spirituality at the same time? Ironically, the answer to the problem of the survival of the planet lies in spirituality as much as it does in politics, science, or economics. Why? And what does that portend for women, for men, for the integrity of spirituality, and the survival of the planet itself?

The domination that lies at the heart of patriarchy lies at the heart of Christianity as well. Derived from an interpretation of creation that is well meaning, perhaps, it is also seriously skewed or, at best, unbalanced beyond redemption. What is construed to be a scripturally given divine mandate for male domination becomes the legitimizing foundation for Christian patriarchy. Created a circle by God, the globe is turned into a pyramid, and the turning is blamed on God.

Exclusionism reigns from the beginning of scriptural history. Gone are the many gods of nature, gone the goddesses of fertility, and in their places not the one God whose name is "I am who am," but man himself astride the universe and, he says, in charge of it.

Even today, a poster in a local day-care center instructs the next generation clearly about the nature, role, and preeminence of men:

Why God Made Little Boys

God made a world out of his dreams,
Of magic mountains, oceans and streams,
Prairies and plains and wooded land,
Then paused and thought,
"I need someone to stand
On top of the mountains to conquer the seas
Explore the plains and climb the trees,
Someone to start out small and grow,
Sturdy, strong like a tree" and so ...
He created boys, full of spirit and fun,
To explore and conquer, to romp and run
With dirty faces, banged-up chins,
With courageous hearts and boyish grins.
When He had completed the task He'd begun,
He surely said,
"That is a job well done."

(Gillian Campbell, 1944)

Boys, a little boy learns young, are created by a male God to "explore and conquer, to romp and run." And romp they do. From one end of life to the other, from the conquest of the playpen to the conquest of the planet, man sees himself in charge.

The justification for the patriarchal thinking and the male god-language found in "Why God Made Little Boys" and bred into both men and women from their earliest years lies in a spiritual tradition interpreted by men to explain, to guarantee, male primacy. Licensing men to "explore and conquer ... with courageous hearts" has its root in selective perception, in taking the major stories of the Judeo-Christian tradition and turning them into a license for rapacious proprietorship rather than a covenant of care.

Of the two creation stories in the Hebrew Scriptures, Genesis 1 and Genesis 2, the philosophers and theologians of the Western world built society on Genesis 1 and failed, obviously, to realize or to teach the enormity of the message in Genesis 2. [92] Clearly, the Judeo-Christian understanding of creation indicates that humans are given responsibility for the earth. The question is whether that responsibility presumes supremacy or stewardship. Patriarchal society concludes that according to Genesis 1 — or for that matter according to the male interpretation of every major creation myth in history — man, males, the apex of creation, can do anything he wants to do with creation for his own good. [93] Feminist society, on the other hand, interprets the relationship of humanity to nature as a compact of accountability, stewardship, responsibility to maintain and develop the Garden in the quality it was given. Why the difference in the interpretation of something so fundamental? Because dominion is only half the Genesis message. Because dominion is a specious message. Because dominion hasn't worked. Every day, as a result of the conquer-and-conquest message, the world comes closer to its own destruction, a situation surely far afield from the purpose of creation.

Genesis 2, the second creation story, the companionship story of creation, commands the human to name the animals. "The man gave names to all cattle," the Scripture reads, "and to the birds of the air, and to every animal of the field...." Clearly, God puts the human in relationship with the rest of creaturehood. But how? Patriarchy says that naming is the process of achieving power over something. To name a thing, this interpretation says, makes a person master of it, superior of it, definer of it. But there is another possible reading, one more common to human relationships in general. It is also true that we name only those things with which we have a personal relationship. To get to know someone's name is to bind ourselves to them in a more personal way. To name something gives it personhood, presence, personality in our sight. Naming a thing does not give me power over it; it simply describes a relationship with something that is more than nothing to me, that has become important to me. It gives the thing named a meaning, a being, a role. It gives it more a power over me than I a power over it. It is the people we know and value whom we call by name. We name our friends. We name those with whom we have a human relationship. We name domestic animals, the ones we come to know as individuals. We name the things with which we have some kind of personal relationship. What we do not name we do not pretend to have feeling for. It's what we don't name that we turn most easily into things. We make objects of them. We deny them personality and autonomy and mutual concern. People do not look an animal in the eye, name it first, and then destroy it. What we bother to name, in other words, we bother to care for. To assume that God brings the animals to Adam to be named so that he can then destroy them as he likes for his own comfort, recreation, and profit denies the very import of naming anything and the rest of the Genesis story along with it.

Immediately after the naming of the animals, the rabbis teach, Yahweh gave very explicit instructions about how to use nature. The humans are told in Genesis 1:18 to eat herbs and fruit and in Genesis 2:15 that they could plow the land but were not to brutalize it. [94] Clearly, the writer of Genesis knows that nature is something to be treated with respect. To cite Scripture as a charter for control, a warrant for degradation, laughs in the face of the God of life. Genesis is the constitution of creation, not of patriarchy. No license here for destruction, exploitation, domination, or ecological bankruptcy in the name of dominion and humanity and the glory of reason.

Nevertheless, thanks to a pathologically anthropomorphic reading of Genesis, Christianity is the most androcentric, most human-centered, most male-privileged of all the major religions on earth. Women, animals, and other living things do not fare well in a world where men, males, assume godlike power and order everything for their own good, to their own comfort, from their own perspective. When the explanation for the situation rests in God, the confusion, the arrogance, the sin are compounded. It is possible that original sin is really original arrogance, the notion that in man and not in the Sabbath — in human maleness rather than in reflection, in insight, in the contemplation of God, in the goodness of life, in praise — lies the crown of creation.

The effects of that kind of thinking abound. They permeate the environment, stratify cultures, separate races, and despoil the earth. Dominant males hoard the goods of the earth; whites enslave people of color economically and socially; men use women for their own ends or admit them to their territory on leashes and in limited numbers. And beyond all that, two hundred million animals are slaughtered every year for medical research alone. The numbers prove the theory: The richest 20 percent of the world's population control over 82 percent of the world's wealth. Only 20 percent of the world's population over the age of 60 have any kind of social security. Almost one billion people — about one-fourth of the population of the earth — already live in areas of severe desertification while the world goes on losing the area of one soccer field per second, and no one does anything about it. The ozone layer, the placenta of the earth, is ruptured; the air we breathe is toxic; the oceans are polluted; the animal species are depleted; the fabric of life is rent and sundered for the poor, exotic and abundant for the rich, absent and out of reach for women, who make up two-thirds of the 850 million illiterates on the globe. [95] As a result, women, in disproportionate numbers, are too uneducated to get jobs, too poor to make a living. They are abandoned, helpless, destitute, undernourished, and denigrated to the point of disdain or patronized to the point of powerlessness, while patriarchy takes dominion and has power over the women, children, animals, elements, oceans, and the very air we breathe. Through it all, the Catholic tradition says that males are meant to rule, and the Protestant tradition says material success is God's reward for virtue and hard work, so the more we have, the more we strive to get. The scene corrupts the meaning of Genesis, sins against creation, begets the ultimate in patriarchal power plays and pyramids. Through it all, a world filled with church-goers is also filled with the obscenely poor. Where are the circles now?

What undergirds such destructive thinking? What does it do to men and women? What kind of spirituality does it spawn? What is its antidote?

Patriarchy is a minefield of inconsistent thinking, of ideas in opposition, of contradictions, of half-truths which destroy the hope for wholeness as it goes. It speaks of wholeness for some but not for all. To repress the insights, the creativity, the presence, the critique, the intellectual otherness of half the human race can not be anything but a crippling blow to human thought, to human decision making, to human ministry. Patriarchy provides the carte blanche for exploitation, a centrifugal force of consumption and abuse that can come to the point where it reasons with blind impunity that a living wage to ensure dignified living conditions, inside plumbing, decent schools, and three meals a day are inappropriate to other cultures. After all, if women are not necessary to the human enterprise and power is the goal, then anyone who differs from the norm, challenges the system, sees from another perspective can be expunged from consideration. There is no such thing as equal. Racism thrives. Sexism abounds. Exploitation is called good business. And militarism flourishes to maintain it.

Patriarchy contrives a system built on the notion that all things exist for the satisfaction of those who can achieve them. It is a system devised by men, for men, and because of men. Women who are privileged by it by virtue of marriage, inheritance, or tokenism, failing to see their own exploitation, are incapable of seeing anyone else's as well and support the system that maintains it. So the system goes on — destructively sexist, inexorably racist, pitiably materialistic, and spiritually bereft — rationalized by philosophy, engendered by theology, fueled by science, and blessed by those who say that God planned the world for the benefit of men. Francis Bacon, the originator of the experimental method, sought scientific knowledge to gain power over nature and based that method on Genesis. "Man fell and lost dominion," Bacon reasoned, but that dominion "can be regained through Scientific study. Nature," Bacon said, "is to be bound into service — like a slave."[96] Science had successfully completed the estrangement of living things: God became remote and transcendent. Nature became a thing. Matter became an object for profit. The economist Malthus, remembered for population studies assumed over time to have been undertaken out of concern for the masses, in 1789 actually opposed the passage of "poor laws" in England. If passed, he warned, they would keep the poor alive and so reduce the wealth of the upper classes. [97] The rush to power had never been greater.

The scientific and philosophical communities, having enthroned reason as the ultimate value in life, declared nature inanimate, devoid of life, worthless — at most the playing field for human power games. Woman, the ultimate symbol of the natural, whose purpose for being was in her body, not her mind, was human, they all agreed, but an inferior facsimile of the real thing. Everything else — rivers and seas, animals and plants, forests and sky — they concluded, was mere instruments of male dominion.

It is a bleak picture, patriarchy, privileging some, oppressing others. In a society such as this, the man who does not kill for sport; who is comfortable with women, seeks them out for their ideas, and promotes them for their insights; who has no need for conspicuous consumption and pays an honest day's wage for an honest day's work is uncomfortable, is out of sync, is in search of a feminist spirituality. A woman who knows the value of her ideas; who learns to insist on being heard; who challenges policies that put the poor, the voiceless, the vulnerable of the human race in jeopardy; who works to restructure all the institutions of society to include her daughters; who is committed to the preservation of the planet is uncomfortable, is out of sync, is in search of a feminist spirituality. Indeed, a new world is coming because it must come, or no decent future, no spiritual authenticity, can be counted on to come at all from the dominion story.

Feminism brings the world back to the companionship story in Genesis. It confronts a system based on androgeny and individual advancement with a system based on communal welfare. It endows the natural with the holy in a world that has moved into cemented cities and has lost contact with, lost respect for, lost a sense of dependence on nature. Feminism puts responsibility for the human race at the center of the economy and profit at the margin. No wonder feminism is such a threat.

A feminist spirituality knows that the ideology of unremitting development and perpetual economic growth is this generation's substitute for fairy tales. An economy fueled by contriving dissatisfaction and converting it into consumerism spins the myth of unlimited progress for the northern hemisphere at the expense of the development of the southern hemisphere. When one world takes the labor, the raw materials, the resources of another world for a pittance and then sells them back to the very people from whom they have been taken for an unconscionable profit — and we do — patriarchy shows one of its uglier faces. The twenty-five largest multinational corporations have annual GNPs that exceed the annual GNPs of the United States and western Europe combined. [98] And all of it in a world without a single international law to govern a single international corporation.

Economics disassociates us from respect for life; politics divorce us from morality; science divorces us from judgment; specialization divorces us from personal responsibility. What is good for the company, what promotes profit, what enhances technology stirs us, drives us, blinds us. Whatever it takes to double the dollar — the squalor of the people, the loss of the rainforests, the weight of the smog, the clogging of waterways, and the appropriation of resources — we leave to the generations to follow with never even the grace to blush. It is business — not government, not law, not morality — that is determining what is appropriate for someone else's culture. It is patriarchy waged in mortal battle for power, profit, and personal supremacy. It is a global male game of ruthless proportions called having dominion and survival of the fittest.

Feminist spirituality says, "Stop!" Feminist spirituality says that in the end we will be judged on the companionship story of Genesis 2. We need a new relationship with animals. We need to immerse ourselves in creation with new respect. We need to come to see ourselves as one more creature dependent on all the others more than they are dependent on us. We need a new sense of enoughness, a new sense of limits, a new sense of interconnectedness with all of life that makes slaughter unthinkable and the destruction of the species impossible. We need to live more simply, take up less space on the earth, and realize the functions of the rest of life so that creation may re-create itself. We need to convert dominion to companionship and patriarchy to feminism before creation itself is in danger from a patriarchy that has admittedly taken science, business, and technology to unparalleled heights but has become pernicious in the process because its tenets are flawed at the core

Finally, feminist spirituality says that feminists themselves must beware. Feminism itself can get trapped in the anthropomorphic, in the human-centered, definition of life. Human-rights feminism, for instance, can idealize autonomy and the freedom to pursue personal ends to such an extent that it limits itself simply to wanting a share in what men already have rather than working to defend the intrinsic value of all things. Radical feminism, a reaction to the sins vented against women, can at its extreme champion a separatism which itself perpetuates patriarchal dualism. Marxist feminism, in its loading of oppression onto economic classism alone, can fail to unmask the patriarchal thinking that makes women and nature the footstools of the human race. Socialist feminism understands both class and gender but pays little or no heed to natural life itself. It resists androgeny, the male-centeredness of society, but, unwittingly at least, leaves anthropomorphism, the human-centeredness of creation, soundly in place in a world in which humans are strangling all life on the globe. Feminism of these types runs the risk of conserving resources for the sake of the survival of the human race rather than for the survival of the planet itself.

We need a feminism based not on femaleness, not on human needs alone, but on a spirituality that is wholistic. Ecofeminism sees the intrinsic value and, therefore, the equal worth of all creation. It draws us beyond ourselves into the preservation of the whole universe. A commitment to the entire web of life in ecofeminism guarantees that we do not become exclusive in our movement toward inclusion. Ecofeminism brings feminism, feminist spirituality, and Genesis itself together in one great burning light, guide to the whole of creation. Ecofeminism is the story of companionship, of responsibility, of accountability for life. All life. Ecofeminism opens the circle and takes the world in on feminist terms.

FEMINISM

....

A REVOLUTION OF THE HEART

He was a young priest, recently ordained and very, very enthusiastic. His first assignment was as chaplain to the local college convent. It was shortly after the opening of Vatican Council II. There was change in the air, and Father knew all about it.

First he would concentrate on the liturgy. And to tell you the truth, it was the liturgy that bothered him most. The sisters came faithfully, but, he noticed to his dismay, they sat scattered around the chapel. Not close. Not like a community of nuns. Not up front where they could be close to the altar. Not where he could speak to them easily as a group. At the end of the first week, he decided to change all that. "Sisters," he said before he left the altar after Mass that morning, "tomorrow I'd like to have everyone sit up here in this section of the chapel, close together and right in front of me." He smiled. No one smiled back, he noticed, but nuns were like that. You could never tell what they were really thinking.

As he turned to leave the sacristy, she was standing in the doorway. She was one of the elders of the community, a woman of substance: tall, white haired, dignified, and strong as stone. "Father," she said without introduction, "we have spent all our lives in this community, wearing what we were told to wear, working at what we were told to do, and sitting where we were told to sit." Her look was straight and clear. She caught his eye and held it with her own. "And we're not going to do that anymore."

He said later that he grew a little that day. Nothing could have made the lesson more clear: There is another world out there waiting to be heard, and they are not going to wait any longer for permission to speak their own truths.

The revolutions that count come silently, come first in the heart, come with the force of steel because they come with no force at all. Revolutions of this magnitude do not overturn a system and then shape it. They reshape thought, and then the system overturns without the firing of a single cannon. Revolutions such as this dismantle walls people thought would never fall because no wall, whatever its size, can contain a people whose minds have long ago scaled and vaulted and surmounted it. It is precisely this kind of tacit revolution which feminism wages in a patriarchal culture, in patriarchal churches right now.

Feminist spirituality challenges the legitimation of arbitrariness, the divine right of power, the holy grail of control, the hegemony of maleness — in both heaven and earth. It shakes the very timbers of history to their base. The forces of reaction swing mightily against it, of course, giving answers that do not silence the obvious questions about the real nature of humanity, about the universal meaning of creation, about a broader set of vision and values. Money, power, and organization array themselves against the forces of change with awesome might. They silence theologians, excommunicate bishops, attack women, rescind legislation, impose sanctions, refuse language changes, control women's wages, and proselytize about the anointed nature of woman's role in a culture shaped by men but ascribed to God. But minds are changing, nevertheless. Public poll after public poll indicates the general acceptance of new relationships, new social roles, new opportunities for women, new parental structures in the workplace for both women and men. Change is coming like a gusher.

What's more, the changes in the air now go far beyond the structure of institutions, the nature of authority, and the deconstruction of old social roles for the sake of fashioning more comfortable ones, though roles just the same. This time change has little to do with institutional tinkering or cosmetic adjustments. It goes far beyond the right to education, the right to vote, the right to legal representation. The changes coming now are far less elementary than that, necessary as those may certainly be to the development of a new worldview. The right to vote is not enough if women do not also have the opportunity to shape the legislation. The right to education is not enough if women never get the chance to change the system. The right to work in the public arena is not enough if women are given neither equal responsibility nor equal pay. It is simply a new form of discrimination. In systems such as these, women stay second place. Women remain reviled. Women become tokens rather than partners. The patriarchal system adjusts to change but maintains its attitudes, its philosophy, its power. But lip service is not enough. We need to refashion society in such a way that women may participate in it without being punished as mothers and wives, as women and professionals. The companies that never think twice about putting in reserve parking lots and golf courses for male executives are going to have to start thinking about putting in day-care centers, flex time, shared time, and home computers, as well. The government must begin to count work done in the home as part of the GNP. We must begin to recognize the presence, the place, and the productivity of the women of the world as well as of the men. We must begin to structure for equality as well as to talk about it.

More than these things, however, the changes emerging in people's hearts now strike at the very roots of society, question its assumptions, challenge its authorities, unmask its sources. The social changes coming now smack of a change in basic attitudes as well as in social conventions. These new attitudes are definitional and essential. They look at women, men, and nature differently. They understand feminism as a distinct worldview rather than a social order. They deal with expectations, not privileges, not gifts, not tokenism, not patronage. They make demands on the basis of a common humanity rather than requests in hope of pity. They stomach no favors. This kind of change rests on the insights of former Attorney General Ramsey Clark, who noted that "a right is not something someone gives you. A right is something that no one can take away." [99] These kinds of changes signal a whole new way of looking at life. These changes signal the emergence of feminism in the face of a patriarchy that has carved up the world for itself and left the human race locked in mortal battle for survival, women the servants of society, and people of color its footstools.

Feminism raises for emulation in the public arena a whole new set of values, a whole new way of relating to others, a whole new way of being woman, being man, a whole new way of defining God, a whole new kind of spirituality. The old order is falling; the old world is over. It may yet be functioning, skeletal and bare, but it is clearly over.

Feminism will not transplant patriarchy by virtue of destroying it. Feminism will survive patriarchy because it exposes its weaknesses, unmasks its failures, and debunks its false promises: Everybody does not get ahead in a patriarchal society; everybody does not have a chance to succeed in a patriarchal society; everybody is not equal in a patriarchal society; every show of force is not justifiable in a patriarchal society; every explanation of God and of life in patriarchy, of good and bad, of the sacred and the mundane, of the holy and the self-righteous does not qualify for Christianity. Feminist spirituality examines the grounds on which patriarchy rests, the goals to which it aspires, the religion it preaches and says, "We're not going to do that anymore."

Feminism makes the display of patriarchal arrogance and patriarchal inconsistency laughable. God is not male, so to insist exclusively on father images for God is laughable. Men are not natural leaders — to wit all the disasters in history — so to assume that, where women and men are concerned, the man must always be the leader is laughable. Reason is not impeccable, not complete, or the history of humanity would not be a history of well-thought-out actions, each of them beneath the divine dimensions of a human race. Force does not assure peace, all the blood feuds in history to the contrary, so to argue that militarism is the way to peace is laughable. Militarism is simply the way to the suppression of dissent, maleness is only half the human race, and God is God, not human, under any circumstances, whatever anybody's narcissistic self-affirmation. God is human only in the Jesus who by virtue of incarnation sanctified all flesh, female and male, and who walked a way that feminists follow with deep feeling, in gentleness, in caring, in honesty, in compassion, and in harmony with the whole of creation.

Feminist spirituality seeks another kind of power, another image of the self, a different relationship with others, and a cosmic view of the world.

Feminist spirituality brings us face to face with the corruptions of power and force and opts for empowerment and nonviolence as the most human responses to the inhuman manipulation of humanity for the sake of the powerful.

What feminist spirituality brings to humankind is the power of nonviolence and the effectiveness of empowerment. What we love we can resist without having to destroy. What we do not set out to destroy we do not meet as enemy. The feminist never wilts in the face of injustice; the feminist simply refuses to become less than fully human. Feminist spirituality resists to the death but never brings death in its wake so that what can be transformed into friendship can be energized for good.

Feminist spirituality looks at pride and strength and finds them wanting in the face of the dignity of humility and the gifts of vulnerability. Feminist spirituality encourages the kind of self-knowledge that recognizes both its strengths and its limitations. It respects the vulnerability that gives a person the capacity for pain. Then, no matter what, I can accept my weaknesses and enjoy my gifts. Then the person of the other, the gifts of the other, are always safe in my presence and sought in my life because I know that it is not necessary to diminish the other in order to magnify myself. I myself am enough for me. A spirituality that opens itself, vulnerable and trusting, to grace as it blows on the wind makes for a world where tears are holy, where human pain is everybody's pain, and where God is a gifting, not an angry, God. Gods made in the image of male potentates are pagan gods at best.

Feminist spirituality measures the effects of competitiveness and authoritarianism and embraces instead compassion and dialogue as the way to human unity.

Feminist spirituality rejects the measuring of the self against the definitions of the other and the absorption of the other into the image and the ambience of those who rule. It gives to everyone the right to be heard, the right to be a person, the right to be self-defining, the right to make mistakes. It defines no one as servant to the creature comforts of another.

Feminist spirituality rejects androgeny and universalism, the notion of male norming, for the sake of otherness, for the sake of the globe. Feminist spirituality accepts otherness as the palette of creation. It seeks its own fulfillment in the gifts of the other. It refuses constricting categories and rigid conventions, social determinants and impermeable boundaries. It embraces the world as part of itself and accepts itself as part of the world, not above it, not below it, but embedded in the heart of creation and sharing its fate. "I will take out of you your stony hearts," God speaks in the Scriptures, "and give you hearts of flesh." I will, in other words, make you human again. I will give you a new way of feeling, a new way of thinking, a new way of being. I will give you another chance to live life in concert with life that ennobles you and does not diminish the other. I will take the pyramid of patriarchy and turn it into a circle where, eye to eye and shoulder to shoulder, you may become a creation full of life, full of god-ness.

It is a complex web, this interweaving of self, of others, of world, and of power. When the configuration begins with the notion of power, then self, others, and world become objects for the use of the powerful. When we justify the objectification of others by blaming the concentration of power on God, then we skew the Scriptures, mock the Jesus who relinquished power, and make power more our god than God. When the filter through which we see the world brings us to openness and compassion for that world — humility in the face of it, vulnerability to the impact of it, nonviolence in dealing with it, and respect for its otherness — then creation is recreated, and humans become human again. When these are the qualities modeled by churches and valued in society, we will have more than religion; we will have Christianity. We may certainly have piety, but we will also have spirituality.

Notes

1 Fraser and Bartky 3–17.
2 Sheldrake 42–44.
3 Russell 36–38.
4 O'Brien and Shannon.
5 Russell 34.
6 Chittister, *A Passion for Life* 95–96.
7 Kenny 107–51.
8 Kenny 107–09.
9 Burke 6.
10 Principe 134.
11 Pius IX, "Quanta Cura" and "Syllabus of Errors"; De Rosa 244–48.
12 O'Faolain and Martines 128–36.
13 Grössman 50–59.
14 Lerner, *The Creation of Feminist Consciousness*.
15 Meredith 90.
16 Maloney 41–49.
17 John Paul II 10–47.
18 Qtd. in Mackinnon and McIntyre 252.
19 Rumi 36.
20 Pascal sec. 24.
21 Aquinas 466–72.
22 Beijing Declaration n.pag.
23 Chittister, *Beyond Beijing* 138–60.
24 Kennedy and Mendus 11.
25 Mendus 33.
26 Kant 167.
27 Rendall 66.
28 Hodge 127.
29 Hodge 134.
30 Canovan 87.
31 Anthony 298–99.
32 Meredith 112.
33 Beaton 17–21.
34 Maccoby and Jacklin.
35 Kenny 186–87.
36 Vare and Ptacek.
37 Eckenstein 42–205.
38 Branden, 74–88.
39 Chittister, *Job's Daughters* 9–31.
40 Rawson 1–13.
41 Hume n.pag.
42 Schaef 104–07, 124–26.
43 Kennedy 181.
44 *Journal of the American Psychosomatic Society* qtd. in *The Electronic Telegraph* n.pag.
45 Source unknown.
46 John XXIII para. 112.

47 Underhill; Sanday 15–51.
48 Dollard et al.
49 Baron and Richardson
   252–62.
50 Baron and Richardson, 265.
51 Baron and Richarson 259.
52 Berkowitz and LePage
   202–07.
53 Bandura.
54 Timpe 33–35.
55 Timpe 34.
56 Coulson 303.
57 King 102–03.
58 Kenny 205.
59 Chittister, *The Rule of Benedict*
   61–74.
60 Pourrat 1: 49.
61 Pourrat 4: 1–37.
62 American Psychiatric
   Association 301–81.
63 Rule of Benedict chap. 7;
   Chittister, *The Rule of Benedict*
   61–75.
64 Kownacki n.pag.
65 Rothman 509–37.
66 Armstrong 102–04.
67 Sheldrake 78.
68 Børresen 170.
69 Børresen 237.
70 William J. Fielding qtd. in
   Dijkstra 4.
71 Irigaray, *I Love to You* 59–68.
72 Eagly; Hillsdale, Erlbaum, and
   Pearson.
73 Bühlmann 143.
74 Rubinstein 237.
75 Adorno.
76 Altemeyer.
77 Cheung and Kwok 333.
78 Altemeyer; Milgram.
79 Melby 99.
80 Jantzen, *Julian of Norwich.*
81 Stone 3–19.
82 Grinyer 26.
83 Brown 35.
84 Jacquelyn Miller 129.
85 Jacquelyn Miller 129.
86 Barker-Benfield in Jacquelyn
   Miller 129.
87 See Burt 343–48; McCollaum
   and Lester 538–39.
88 Altman and Taylor.
89 Sherif and Sherif 382–417.
90 Allport 138–58.
91 Weber 152–53.
92 Ruether 1–32; Perry.
93 Carmody; Chittister,
   *Militarism, Sexism, and
   Theology.*
94 Weiss n.pag.
95 Tavis 3–25.
96 Clifford 340.
97 Clifford 342.
98 Fox-Genovese 235.
99 Clark.

SELECTED BIBLIOGRAPHY

Adorno, Theodor. *The Authoritarian Personality*. New York: Norton, 1950.

Agonito, Rosemary. *History of Ideas on Women: A Source Book*. New York: Perigee-Putnam's, 1977.

Allport, Gordon W. *The Nature of Prejudice*. Garden City: Anchor-Doubleday, 1958.

Altemeyer, B. *Enemies of Freedom: Understanding Right-Wing Authoritarianism*. San Francisco: Jossey-Bass, 1988.

Altman, I., and D.A. Taylor. *Social Penetration: The Development of Interpersonal Relationships*. New York: Holt, 1973.

American Psychiatric Association. Work Group to Revise DSM III. *Diagnostic and Statistical Manual of Mental Disorders*. 3rd ed., rev. Washington, DC: American Psychiatric, 1987.

Anderson, Bonnie S., and Judith P. Zinsser. *A History of Their Own: Women in Europe from Prehistory to the Present*. 2 vols. New York: Harper, 1988.

Anthony, Katherine. *Susan B. Anthony: Her Personal History and Her Era*. Garden City, NY: Doubleday, 1954.

Aquinas, Thomas. *Summa Theologica*. New York: Benziger, 1947.

Armstrong, Karen. *A History of God: The 4000-Year Quest of Judaism, Christianity, and Islam*. New York: Knopf, 1993.

Barker-Benfield, G.J. *The Culture of Sensibility: Sex and Society in Eighteenth-Century Britain*. Chicago: U of Chicago P, 1992.

Bandura, Albert. *Aggression: A Social Learning Analysis*. Englewood Cliffs, NJ: Prentice, 1973.

Baron, Robert A., and Deborah R. Richardson. *Human Aggression*. 2nd ed. New York: Plenum, 1994.

Beaton, Catherine. "Does the Church Discriminate Against Women on the Basis of Their Sex?" *The Critic* June-July 1966: 17–21.

Beijing Declaration. *Fourth World Conference on Women.* New York: United Nations, 1995. A/Conf. L.1, English.

Bem, Sandra. *The Lenses of Gender.* New Haven: Yale UP, 1993.

Benhabib, Seyla. *Situating the Self: Gender, Community, and Postmodernism in Contemporary Ethics.* London: Polity, 1992.

Benhabib, Seyla, Judith Butler, Drucilla Cornell, and Nancy Fraser. *Feminist Contentions: A Philosophical Exchange.* New York: Routledge, 1995.

Berelson, Bernard, and Gary A. Steiner. *Human Behavior: An Inventory of Scientific Findings.* New York: Harcourt, 1964.

Berkowitz, Leonard. *Aggression.* New York: McGraw-Hill, 1962.

Berkowitz, Leonard, and A. LePage. "Weapons as Aggression-Eliciting Stimuli." *Journal of Personality and Social Psychology* 7.1 (1967): 202–07.

Bock, Gisela, and Susan James, eds. *Beyond Equality and Difference: Citizenship, Feminist Politics, and Female Subjectivity.* New York: Routledge, 1992.

Borg, Marcus E. *A New Vision of Jesus.* San Francisco: HarperCollins, 1991.

Børresen, Kari Elisabeth, ed. *The Image of God: Gender Models in the Judaeo-Christian Tradition.* Minneapolis: Fortress, 1995.

Braidotti, Rosie. *Patterns of Dissonance: A Study of Women in Contemporary Philosophy.* London: Polity, 1991.

Branden, Nathaniel. *The Psychology of Self-Esteem.* Los Angeles: Nash, 1969.

Brown, Stuart. "Concepts of Childhood and Play." *ReVision* 17 (1995): 35.

– – – . "An Interview with Brian Sutton-Smith." *ReVision* 17 (1995): 35.

Bühlmann, Walbert. *The Coming of the Third Church.* Maryknoll, NY: Orbis, 1978.

Burke, Vernon J. "Augustine of Hippo: The Approach of the Soul to God." *Spirituality of Western Christendom.* Ed. E. Rozanne Elder. Kalamazoo, MI: Cistercian, 1976. 1–12.

Burt, M. "Cultural Myths and Support for Rape." *Journal of Personality and Social Psychology* 38.2 (1980): 217–30.

Butler, D., and F.L. Geis. "Nonverbal Affect Responses to Male and Female Leaders: Implications for Leadership Evaluations." *Journal of Personality and Social Psychology* 58.1 (1990): 48–59.

Butler, Judith. *Gender Trouble, Feminism, and the Subversion of Identity.* New York: Routledge, 1990.

Canovan, Margaret. "Rousseau's Two Concepts of Citizenship." Kennedy and Mendus 78–105.

Carmody, Denise. *Women and World Religions.* Englewood Cliffs, NJ: Prentice-Hall, 1988.

Carr, Anne E. *Transforming Grace: Christian Tradition and Women's Experience*. San Francisco: Harper, 1988.

Carr, Anne E., and Elizabeth Schüssler Fiorenza, eds. *The Special Nature of Women?* London: SCM, 1991.

Cheung, Chau-Kiu, and Sin-Tong Kwok. "Conservative Orientation as a Determinant of Hopelessness." *Journal of Social Psychology* 136 (1996): 333–47.

Chittister, Joan. *Job's Daughters: Women and Power*. New York: Paulist, 1990.

– – – . *A Passion for Life*. Maryknoll, NY: Orbis, 1996.

– – – . *The Rule of Benedict: Insights for the Ages*. New York: Crossroad, 1992.

– – – . *Beyond Beijing: The Next Step for Women*. Kansas City, MO: Sheed, 1996.

Christ, Carol P., and Judith Plaskow, eds. *Womanspirit Rising: A Feminist Reader in Religion*. San Francisco: HarperCollins, 1979.

Clark, Ramsey. *New York Times* 2 Oct. 1977.

Clifford, Anne M. "Feminist Perspectives on Science: Implications for an Ecological Theology of Creation." MacKinnon and McIntyre 334–60.

Coakley, Sarah. "Creaturehood Before God: Male and Female." *Theology* 93 (1990): 343–54.

Condren, Mary. *The Serpent and the Goddess: Women, Religion, and Power in Celtic Ireland*. San Francisco: HarperCollins, 1989.

Confoy, Maryanne, Dorothy A. Lee, and Joan Nowotny. *Freedom and Entrapment*. Victoria, Austral.: Dove-HarperCollins, 1995.

Conn, Joann Wolski., ed. *Women's Spirituality: Resources for Christian Development*. New York: Paulist, 1986.

Cooey, Paula M., William R. Eakin, and Jay B. McDaniel, eds. *After Patriarchy: Feminist Transformations of the World Religions*. Faith Meets Faith Series. Maryknoll, NY: Orbis, 1991.

Coulson, John, ed. *The Saints: A Concise Biographical Dictionary*. New York: Hawthorn, 1958.

Crossan, John Dominic. *Jesus: A Revolutionary Biography*. San Francisco: HarperCollins, 1994.

Cunneen, Sally. *In Search of Mary, the Woman and the Symbol*. New York: Ballantine-Random, 1995.

De Rosa, Peter. *Vicars of Christ: The Dark Side of the Papacy*. New York: Crown, 1988.

Dijkstra, Bram. *Evil Sisters: The Threat of Female Sexuality and the Cult of Manhood*. New York: Knopf, 1996.

Dollard, J., L.W. Doob, N.E. Miller, O.H. Mowrer, and R.R. Sears. *Frustration and Aggression*. New Haven: Yale UP, 1939.

Donovan, Josephine. *Feminist Theory: The Intellectual Traditions of American Feminism*. New York: Ungar, 1986.

Eagly, Alice Hendrickson. *Sex Differences in Social Behavior: A Social-Role Interpretation*. Hillsdale, NJ: Erlbaum, 1987.

Eckenstein, Lina. *Woman under Monasticism*. Cambridge, UK: 1896.

Eisenstein, Hester. *Contemporary Feminist Thought*. London: Unwin, 1984.

Elder, E. Rozanne, ed. *The Spirituality of Western Christendom*. Kalamazoo, MI: Cistercian, 1976.

– – – . *The Roots of the Modern Christian Tradition*. Kalamazoo, MI: Cistercian, 1984.

Elwes, Teresa, ed. *Women's Voices: Essays in Contemporary Feminist Theology*. London: Pickering, 1992.

Foucault, M. *The History of Sexuality III: The Care of the Self*. Trans. R. Hurley. New York: Pantheon, 1984.

Fox-Genovese, Elizabeth. "From Separate Spheres to Dangerous Streets: Postmodernist Feminism and the Problem of Order." *Social Research* 60 (1993): 235–54.

Fraser, Nancy, and Sandra Lee Bartky, eds. *Revaluing French Feminism: Critical Essays on Difference, Agency, and Culture*. Bloomington: Indiana UP, 1992.

Fuss, Diane. *Essentially Speaking: Feminism, Nature, and Difference*. London: Routledge, 1989.

Gatens, Moira. *Feminism and Philosophy: Perspectives on Difference and Equality*. Bloomington: Indiana UP, 1991.

Grinyer, Peter. "A Cognitive Approach to Facilitating Group Decision Taking: Analysis of Practice." *Knowledge and Policy* 5 (1992): 26.

Grössman, Elizabeth. "The Construction of Women's Difference in the Christian Theological Tradition." Carr and Fiorenza 50–59.

Grosz, Elizabeth. "The Hetero and the Homo: The Sexual Ethics of Luce Irigaray." *Gay Information* no. 17–18 (1987): 37–44.

Hampson, Daphne, ed. *Swallowing a Fishbone: Feminist Theologians Debate Christianity*. London: Society for Promoting Christian Knowledge (SPCK), 1996.

Heilbrun, Carolyn G. *Reinventing Womanhood*. New York: Norton, 1979.

Hillsdale, M.J., Lawrence Erlbaum, and J.C. Pearson. *Gender and Communication*. Dubuque, IA: Brown, 1985.

Hodge, Joanna. "Women and the Hegelian State." Kennedy and Mendus 127–58.

Horney, Karen. *The Neurotic Personality of Our Time.* New York: Norton, 1937.

Hume, David. "Signing of the Magna Carta." *History of the World.* Bureau of Electronic Publishing, Inc., 1992. 1 Jan. 1992.

International Encyclopedia of Psychiatry, Psychology, Psychoanalysis, and Neurology. Ed. Benjamin B. Wolman. New York: Van Nostrand, 1977. 1:329–56.

Irigaray, Luce. *An Ethics of Sexual Difference.* Trans. C. Burke and G. C. Gill. London: Athlone, 1993.

– – – . *I Love to You: Sketch for a Felicity within History.* Trans. Alison Martin. New York: Routledge, 1996.

Jantzen, Grace M. "Feminists, Philosophers, and Mystics." *Hypatia* 9.4 (1994): 186–205.

– – – . *Julian of Norwich: Mystic and Theologian.* New York, Paulist, 1988.

John XXIII. *Pacem in Terris.* Vatican City: Vatican Polyglot, 1963.

John Paul II. "Mulieres Dignitatem." *The Pope Speaks* 34 (1989–90): 10–47.

Johnson, Elizabeth A. *She Who Is: The Mystery of God in Feminist Theological Discourse.* New York: Crossroad, 1992.

Jones, Cheslyn, Geoffrey Wainwright, and Edward Yarnold, eds. *The Study of Spirituality.* London: SPCK, 1992.

Joseph, Alison, ed. *Through the Devil's Gateway: Women, Religion, and Taboo.* London: SPCK, 1990.

Journal of the American Psychosomatic Society. Qtd. in *The Electronic Telegraph.* London 23 Jan. 1997.

Kant, Immanuel. *Anthropology from a Pragmatic Point of View.* Trans. Mary Gregor. The Hague: Nijhoff, 1974.

Kaufmann, Harry. *Aggression and Altruism: A Psychological Analysis.* Austin, TX: Rinehart, 1970.

Kennedy, Ellen, and Susan Mendus, eds. *Women in Western Political Philosophy: Kant to Nietzsche.* Brighton, UK: Wheatsheaf, 1987.

Kenny, Anthony, ed. *The Oxford History of Western Philosophy.* Oxford, UK: Oxford UP, 1994.

Kidd, Susan Monk. *Dance of a Dissident Daughter.* San Francisco: HarperSan Francisco, 1996.

Kim, C.W. Maggie, Susan M. St. Ville, and Susan M. Simonaitis, eds. *Transfigurations, Theology, and the French Feminists.* Minneapolis: Fortress, 1993.

King, Martin Luther, Jr. *Stride Toward Freedom.* San Francisco: Harper, 1958.

King, Ursula. *Women and Spirituality: Voice of Protest and Promise.* 2nd ed. London: Macmillan, 1993.

– – – , ed. *Feminist Theology from the Third World: A Reader.* Maryknoll, NY: Orbis; London: SPCK, 1994.

Kownacki, Mary Lou. *The Sacred in the Simple: Making Mantras Part of Christian Living.* Liguori, MO: Liguori, 1995.

LaCugna, Catherine, ed. *Freeing Theology.* San Francisco: Harper, 1993.

Leonard, Richard. *Beloved Daughters: 100 Years of Papal Women.* Melbourne, Austral.: Lovell, 1995.

Lerner, Gerda. *The Majority Finds Its Past: Placing Women in History.* New York: Oxford UP, 1981.

– – – . *The Creation of Patriarchy.* New York: Oxford UP, 1986.

– – – . *The Creation of Feminist Consciousness.* New York: Oxford UP, 1993.

Lerner, Michael. *The Politics of Meaning.* New York: Addison-Wesley, 1996.

Loades, Ann. *Feminist Theology: A Reader.* London: SPCK, 1990.

Lorenz, Konrad. *On Aggression.* New York: Harcourt, 1966.

Maccoby, E., and C. Jacklin. *The Psychology of Sex Differences.* Stanford, CA: Stanford UP, 1974.

MacKinnon, Mary Heather, and Moni McIntyre, eds. *Readings in Ecology and Feminist Theology.* Kansas City, MO: Sheed, 1995.

Maitland, Sarah. *A Map of the New Country: Women and Christianity.* London: Routledge, 1991.

Maloney, Linda M. "The Argument for Women's Difference in Classical Philosophy and Early Christianity." Carr and Fiorenza 41–49.

McCollaum, Bruce, and David Lester. "Sexual Aggression and Attitudes Toward Women and Mothers." *The Journal of Social Psychology* 137 (1997): 538–39.

McFague, Sallie. *The Body of God: An Ecological Theology.* Minneapolis: Fortress, 1993.

McGinn, Bernard, John Meyendorff, and Jean Leclercq, eds. *Christian Spirituality: Origins to the Twelfth Century.* New York: Crossroad, 1989.

Melby, Ernest O. "Authoritarianism: Enslaving Yoke of Nations and Schools." *Clearing House* 1 Nov. 1995: 99.

Mendus, Susan. "Kant: 'An Honest but Narrow-Minded Bourgeois'?" Kennedy and Mendus 1–20.

Merchant, Carolyn. *The Death of Nature: Women, Ecology, and the Scientific Revolution.* San Francisco: Harper, 1980.

Meredith, Anthony. "Greek Philosophy, Wisdom Literature, and Gnosis." Jones, Wainwright, and Yarnold 90–94.

Milgram, Stanley. *Obedience to Authority*. New York: Harper, 1974.

Miller, Jacquelyn. "An 'Uncommon Tranquility of Mind': Emotional Self-Control in the Construction of a Middle-Class Identity in Eighteenth-Century Philadelphia." *Journal of Social History* 30 (1996): 129–48.

Miller, Jean Baker. *Toward a New Psychology of Women*. Boston: Beacon, 1976.

Mollenkott, V.R. *The Divine Feminine: The Biblical Imagery of God as Female*. New York: Crossroad, 1983.

Montagu, Ashley. *The Nature of Human Aggression*. New York: Oxford UP, 1976.

New Dictionary of Catholic Spirituality, The. 2 vols. Ed. Michael Downey. Collegeville, MN: Liturgical, 1993.

O'Brien, David, and Thomas A. Shannon. *Catholic Social Thought: The Documentary Heritage*. Maryknoll, NY: Orbis, 1992.

O'Faolain, Julia, and Lauro Martines, eds. *Not in God's Image: Women in History from the Greeks to the Victorians*. New York: Harper, 1973.

Othman, Norami, and Cecelia Ng Choon Sim, eds. *Gender, Culture, and Religion*. Kuala Lumpur: Persatuan Saans Sosial Malaysia, 1995.

Pascal, Blaise. *Pensees*. New York: Viking-Penguin, 1995.

Pateman, Carole, and Elizabeth Gross. *Feminist Challenges: Social and Political Theory*. Boston: Northeastern UP, 1986.

Perry, John Michael. *Creation*. Kansas City, MO: Sheed, 1992.

Pius IX. "Quanta Cura." *Catholic Encyclopedia*. New York: Encyclopedia, 1913. New Advent, 1996.

– – – . "Syllabus of Errors." *Catholic Encyclopedia*. New York: Encyclopedia, 1913. New Advent, 1996.

Pourrat, Pierre. *Christian Spirituality*. 4 vols. Westminster, MD: Newman, 1953.

Principe, Walter. "Towards Defining Spirituality." *Studies in Religion* 12 (1983):127–41.

Raison, Beryl. *The Family in Ancient Rome: New Perspectives*. Ithaca, NY: Cornell UP, 1986.

Raitt, Jill, Bernard McGinn, and John Meyendorff. *Christian Spirituality II: High Middle Ages and Reformation*. New York: Crossroad, 1987.

Randour, Mary Lou. *Women's Psyche, Women's Spirit: The Reality of Relationships*. New York: Columbia UP, 1987.

Rawson, Beryl, ed. *The Family in Ancient Rome*. Ithaca: Cornell UP, 1986. 1–13.

Reardon, Kathleen. *They Don't Get It, Do They?* New York: Little-Brown, 1995.

Rendall, Jane. "Virtue and Commerce: Women in the Making of Adam Smith's Political Economy." Kennedy and Mendus 21–44.

Rothman, Stanley. "American Entrepreneurship: Its Rise and Decline." *The World and I* Nov. 1991: 509–37.

Rubinstein, Gidi. "Authoritarianism in Israeli Society." *Journal of Social Psychology* 135 (1995): 237.

Ruether, Rosemary Radford. "Being a Catholic Feminist at the End of the Twentieth Century." *Feminist Theology* 1 (1992): 9–20.

– – – . *Gaia and God: An Ecofeminist Theology of Earth Healing.* San Francisco: HarperCollins, 1992.

Rumi. *The Essential Rumi.* Trans. Coleman Barks and John Moyne. San Francisco: HarperCollins, 1995.

Russell, Anthony. "Sociology and the Study of Spirituality." Jones, Wainwright, and Yarnold 33–38.

Sanday, Peggy Reeves. *Female Power and Male Dominance: On the Origins of Sexual Inequality.* London: Cambridge UP, 1981.

Schaef, Anne Wilson. *Women's Reality: An Emerging Female System in the White Male Society.* Minneapolis: Winston, 1981.

Schottroff, Luise. *Lydia's Impatient Sisters: A Feminist Social History of Early Christianity.* London: SCM, 1995.

Sheldrake, Philip. *Spirituality and History.* 2nd ed. London: SPCK, 1995.

Sherif, Muzafer, and Carolyn W. Sherif. *Social Psychology.* New York: Harper, 1969.

Soskice, Janet. "Christ in Feminist Context." *Christ and Context.* Ed. H. Regan. Edinboro: Clark, 1993.

– – – . "Trinity and the 'Feminine Other.'" *New Blackfriars* 75 (1994): 2–17.

Spretnak, Charlene. *States of Grace: The Recovery of Meaning in the Postmodern Age.* San Francisco: HarperSan Francisco, 1991.

Stone, W. F. "The Myth of Left-Wing Authoritarianism." *Political Psychology* 19 Mar. 1980: 3–19.

Swimme, Brian, and Thomas Berry. *The Universe Story.* New York: HarperCollins, 1992.

Tavis, Lee A. *Power and Responsibility: Multinational Managers and Developing Country Concerns.* Notre Dame, IN: U of Notre Dame P, 1997.

Timpe, R.L. "Aggression." *Baker Encyclopedia of Psychology.* Ed. David G. Benner. Grand Rapids, MI: Baker, 1985.

Tong, Rosemarie. *Feminist Thought: A Comprehensive Introduction*. Boulder: Westview, 1989.

Tuana, Nancy. *Woman and the History of Philosophy*. New York: Paragon, 1992.

Underhill, Ruth M. "Eskimo." *Colliers Encyclopedia*. CD-ROM. 2 Feb. 1996.

Vare, Ethlie, and Greg Ptacek. *Mothers of Invention: From the Bra to the Bomb: Forgotten Women and Their Unforgettable Ideas*. New York: Morrow, 1989.

Warren, Karen J., ed. *Ecological Feminist Philosophies*. Bloomington, IN: Indiana UP, 1996.

Weber, Max. *The Theory of Social and Economic Organization*. Ed. Talcott Parsons. New York: Free, 1947.

Weiss, Avi. "Tu B'Shevat: A Day to Contemplate Ecological Responsibilities." *MetroWest Jewish News*. Stamford: CT: Ethnic NewsWatch. Softline Information Inc., 12 Jan. 1995.

Welch, Charon D. *A Feminist Ethic of Risk*. Minneapolis: Fortress, 1990.

West, Angel. *Deadly Innocence: Feminism and the Mythology of Sin*. London: Mowbray, 1995.

Williams, D.G., and Gabrielle Morris. "Crying, Weeping, or Tearfulness in British and Israeli Adults." *British Journal of Psychology* 87 (1996): 479.

Woolf, Virginia. A Room of One's Own *and* Three Guineas. Oxford: Oxford UP, 1992.

Zappone, Katherine E. "The Faith of Feminists: Charting 'New Territory.'" Devlin Lecture. University of St. Jerome's College. Waterloo, ON, 14 Nov. 1994.

– – – . *The Hope for Wholeness: A Spirituality for Feminists*. Mystic, CT: Twenty-Third, 1991.

Colophon

....

....

Type was set in 11-point Goudy Old Style on 13-point leading. This book was produced by Aaron Phipps with a Power Macintosh 7100/66 computer using Quark XPress 3.31. Transparencies of original art were transferred to Kodak's Pro Photo CD and prepared for printing with Adobe Photoshop 4.0 software.

†